STATES

Gulf of Mexico

Atlantic Ocean

Campeche

Caribbean Sea

HAITI

JAMAICA

GUATEMALA

BRITISH HONDURAS

HONDURAS

SALVADOR

NICARAGUA

COSTA RICA

Pacific Ocean

PANAMA

Gulf of Panama

COLOMBIA

BLATTNER

"The vast territory of Mexico and the five republics which constitute the region known as Central America may be regarded as a single region forming a sub-continent, a narrowed continuation of North America. . . . Through this region a broad and lofty mountain mass curves from northwest to southeast, so that the products of every climate can flourish at different heights in the same latitude: the torrid coastal strips, typically tropical in climate, bordering the shores of both oceans; the beautiful, wholesome and productive country of long upland valleys and level spaces between the mountains; and finally, towering above these, the chilly inhospitable region of the great heights." — Kirkpatrick.

LIBERATORS AND HEROES OF MEXICO AND CENTRAL AMERICA

BOOKS BY MARION F. LANSING

LIBERATORS AND HEROES OF SOUTH AMERICA

LIBERATORS AND HEROES OF MEXICO AND
CENTRAL AMERICA

HIDALGO AT THE HEAD OF HIS ARMY
(See page 27)

LIBERATORS
and HEROES of
MEXICO and
CENTRAL AMERICA

☆ ☆ ☆ ☆

by

MARION
LANSING

Jacket in color by Robert Blattner

L. C. Page & Company
Publishers · Boston

"Comprehension must be the soil in which shall grow all the fruits of friendship."

PREFACE

Every once in a while some happening of the present turns our interest on a period of the past, as if a searchlight was thrown upon it. So it is today with the period more than one hundred years ago when the American colonies which had been a part of Spain's empire freed themselves from overseas control, as the British colonies had freed themselves a generation earlier. It mattered much to us in the United States during that first quarter of the nineteenth century that these nearby countries should so separate themselves, and their statesmen and ours dreamed dreams of a continental, or inter-continental, unity for purposes of defense and trade. Most of all, we all shared a passion for independence and were willing to try out new experiments in government and test new theories of the rights of man to see if they could be made to work.

With the first act of the drama of the winning of independence by the Americas, which is our own nation's story, we are wholly familiar. With the South American Wars of Independence, led a generation later by Bolívar and San Martín, we have what might be called a speaking acquaintance. But of the Mexican and Central American scenes in the drama, most of us have little knowledge. Yet their own Independence Days are as precious

—: vii :—

to the people of these republics to the south of us as are our national days to us, and the names of their heroes are as proudly remembered.

In these countries there is a pleasant custom of honoring such men by naming them, in Congress duly assembled and with all formality, *Benemérito de la Patria,* "Well-deserving of the Fatherland," and so it is with these men whose stories we have chosen to tell. They were so selected for us by the people whom they represent, the leading six, the Indian democrat, Juarez of Mexico, the reformer, Barrios of Guatemala, the pioneer patriot, Delgado of El Salvador, the fighting general, Morazán of Honduras, Mora, the defender of Costa Rica, and Larreinaga, the jurist of Nicaragua, being chosen as their nations' heroes for the Pan American Gallery of Patriots, in Washington, D. C. With them are the men like Hidalgo of Mexico, who sounded the first call to independence, Valle of Salvador who wrote the Central American Declaration of Independence of 1821, Father Simeon Canas who wrote into the constitution of 1823 the first provision for the abolition of slavery in the modern world, and others who shared in the building of the new republics.

They are a group for Americans to be proud of, these men who faced almost insuperable obstacles and were not daunted. The untrained peoples whom they tried to lead were not ready for the responsibilities of self-government and fell too easily into the hands of ambitious dictators.

It took a century for their dreams of agriculture, public education, and connecting highways to come within sight of accomplishment. Yet these men set the pattern which the leaders of today are working out. Chiefly, however, they are remembered, as are the heroes of every country and every age, for their daring, their devotion, and the gallant deeds which we have here endeavored to chronicle.

The record of their lives is not easily found out. The search leads to almost forgotten diaries of travel, to precious memorials printed in their own countries at the time of their death, or on the occasion of the dedication of a statue or a university building or of a centenary. We are indebted to the Harvard College Library and the Boston Athenaeum for access to valuable sources, and to the Pan American Union in Washington for its "Pan American Patriots Series" and especially for the "Bulletin," published monthly for these many years, in the articles of which distinguished writers of the different countries have given the national estimates of these men. Nor can one fail to mention the many scholarly histories written by American students of Latin American backgrounds.

It has been possible only to touch on the lives of these men and the situations in which they found themselves, and no one can be more conscious than we of the limitations of such a survey. Yet we hope to have shared our growing interest in these men who cherished so many of our national hopes and ideals. Their ways are different from our ways, but students wiser than we see here the working out of American patterns for the future. It would be a pity for us to miss the thrill of these chapters in the drama of American independence or fail to know these courageous pioneers.

M. L.

Cambridge, Massachusetts
September, 1941.

—: x :—

CONTENTS

CONTENTS

CONTENTS

CONTENTS

CONTENTS

CONTENTS

—: xvi :—

ILLUSTRATIONS

ILLUSTRATIONS

LIBERATORS AND HEROES
OF MEXICO
AND CENTRAL AMERICA

THE PARTING OF THE WAYS

ON the fifteenth of September each year, a few minutes before midnight, the President of the Republic of Mexico stands forth before an assembled multitude of people in the National Palace in Mexico City and pulls a rope that rings a church bell hanging there. By that act and in the words of the proclamation which follows, he is rejoicing once more in the independence of the nation, and ushering in the glorious Sixteenth of September, patriot day for all Mexico, on which the people celebrate the beginning, early in the nineteenth century, of their separate national life.

It is an old bell, a small one, such as hung in the belfries of churches all over Mexico and Central America in those years. But by the use to which it was put on that long-ago September of 1810, it became the "Liberty Bell" of Mexico. When its note sounds forth at the President's call, those who listen are seeing it as it hung in the little village church of Dolores, and are remembering a midnight ride to the home of a village priest. That ride is as much a part of Mexico's life as the ride of Paul

Revere to Lexington and Concord in our own American Revolution. The sound of that bell recalls a signal given by a high-bred patriot lady, three taps on her bedroom floor in the government house, which gave warning of an independence plot discovered too soon and of patriots arrested. Those who gather each year to hear the "Liberty Bell" rung once more are giving honor to the village priest who led this revolution of 1810, Miguel Hidalgo, "Father of Mexican Independence."

AMERICA FREES ITSELF

It has always been our American custom to make much of the stories which have come down to us of the winning of freedom. Every step along the path to freedom and democracy which was taken in the Old World has been cherished, every national hero honored. But the tales of the freeing of the other Americas from Spanish rule have failed, until recently, to become a part of our North American tradition. It has taken the new sense of the Americas as a unit to bring home to us the importance of the movements in Mexico, Central America, and South America which completed the separation from the Old World which our own American Revolution had begun.

The South American story is an epic of war, with twenty years of bitter fighting before the Spanish armies were defeated and the Spanish ruling officials driven from the continent. In that struggle we of the North American continent had little part, save as onlookers.

—: 4 :—

Mexico and Central America were nearer, and their history runs more parallel to our own. In the years when the newborn republics were trying to establish themselves, our sea captains were in their ports, our adventurers were visiting their cities and exploring their territory, and our statesmen and theirs were discussing the possibilities of a United America. We were delighted to have them freeing themselves from European rule, and watched anxiously their successes or failures in their new form of government.

IN CENTRAL AMERICA

Matching the Independence Day of Mexico of 1810 there is a September day of 1821 for Central America, when a group of distinguished leaders of the provinces which were part of Spain's great empire met in Guatemala City to debate the issue of freedom. Here the picture is of a group of men rather than a single outstanding figure. It is of a Congress, not unlike our own Continental Congress, which met in the early morning to vote whether a Declaraton of Independence should be adopted. As on our own Independence Day in Philadelphia in 1776, there was an eager crowd waiting outside the assembly hall. As the hours passed, more and more people packed the courtyard and the balconies, waiting for the news. When the word came that the delegates had voted for the Declaration, a shout went up. Could it be that three hundred years of Spanish rule were to be ended by a single vote? Would the five provinces back up this action taken in Guatemala City, when the news was carried over mountain paths and along narrow roads through forests and jungles to the cities of El Salvador and Honduras, Nicaragua and Costa Rica, and back into the more remote regions of Guatemala? The answer is given in the story of the lives of the men whom the five republics remember with honor as they celebrate each year the September day which marks the beginning of their freedom from Old World rule.

WHY THE MEXICAN REVOLUTION?

Spain did not deserve to hold its empire in the New World, and especially the kings of Spain did not deserve any credit for their colonial policy during the last years of the eighteenth century and the opening decade of the nineteenth. They were living, as were the other kings of Europe, in an Old World, a world patterned on the fashion of the earlier Middle Ages.

There is a statement made by the Viceroy of New Spain in the year 1767 which shows their attitude. "Once and for all, and for the future," he declared, as he repeated one of his royal master's orders, "the vassals of the Great Monarch who occupies the throne of Spain must know that they were born to hold their tongues and to obey, and not to discuss, nor express opinions on high matters of State." The colonies were the personal possession of the kings, and they treated them as such, getting from them all the moneys they could, and giving as little in the way of self-government as could be managed.

A century earlier they might have succeeded; but now the idea of independence was in the air. The North American colonies were freeing themselves from British rule; the French Revolution was in progress, and the writings of French philosophers who stood for the rights of the common man came into the colonies on every boat. It was useless for Crown or Church to try to keep these ideas out, though both tried by every means. Governing officials were sternly warned "not to let anything enter the colonies which might suggest either revolt or independence." The Church forbade the reading of modern books and set up courts before which any person suspected of liberal ideas was brought and questioned. Yet the stories of the patriots, as we shall read them, show how utterly all these measures failed. Only a Robinson Crusoe alone on a desert island could have failed to catch the spirit of the age and respond to it with either enthusiasm or hatred.

WRONGS THAT NEEDED RIGHTING

In Mexico in these years there was a growing ill-feeling between different classes. Here as in all Spanish American colonies the Creoles were desperately jealous of the men from Spain to whom went all the good positions in the government. These Creoles were native Americans of Spanish family and ancestry. Only the fact of living in Mexico, of having been born there, stood between them and the coveted offices; but proud young men of noble family and excellent education found themselves socially on a lower level than the newest arrival from Spain.

The first uprising against the Spanish rule came from this injustice. Eleven years before the Hidalgo revolt, back in 1799, there was a Creole conspiracy in which the cry was "Death to the Spaniards! Away with the Spaniards!" The plotters were armed with only a few machetes (sabers) and had neither money nor adequate backing for success. But the wise Viceroy, Miguel de Azanza, who dealt with the rebels, was deeply troubled.

"By some misfortune," he reported to his home government, "there exists in America an ancient division, a bitter enmity, between Europeans and Creoles, an enmity capable of producing the most fatal results and which must ever be a source of apprehension to the government."

If Mexico had been a backward colony, there might have been some excuse for such treatment of the native-born; but back of its life lay three hundred years of history. Mexico City was not only the largest city on either American continent, but one of the finest on either side of the Atlantic. Of it the historian Bancroft says that its buildings were finer than those in many Spanish cities, the native stones of which they were constructed giving them an "aspect of solidity and splendor." It was a well-kept city, too, with an enviable reputation for cleanliness in a time when many cities were danger-spots for the spread of disease. Under energetic viceroys of the last years of the eighteenth century, there had been the paving of the main streets and the putting in of oil lamps. Police patrolled the main avenues, and street-sweepers went back and forth along them with their hand carts. This capital of New Spain was a city of which its natives might well be proud. For its natives to be looked down upon by governing officials from Spain became in these years a source of increasing bitterness.

Another, and a constant, evil was the oppression of the Indians. The wiser Spanish officials did not fail to inform the king and his council of the dangers that went with this state of affairs. The Bishop of Michoacan, the province adjoining Mexico City on the west, wrote in 1799 a long memorial calling his sovereign's attention to the condition of his humbler subjects. The Indians, he said, and the mixed races, making up nine-tenths of the entire population, till the soil, work the mines, and carry on all the labor of the country, while the Spaniards own nearly all the property. Out of such a condition, wrote the wise bishop, may be easily born that hatred between "those who have everything and those who have nothing, between owners and slaves." The sufferings of the Indians, their ignorance, and above all their misery placed them at an enormous distance from the whites. Both Indians and mixed races were "in a most humiliating position."

"This being the situation," the bishop warned his king, "what loyalty can the Indians, despised, degraded, almost propertyless and with no hope of bettering themselves, feel for the government? . . . If new legislation does not take into account the lot of the Indians and people of color, the ascendancy of the clergy, however great it may be over the hearts of these unfortunates, will not be sufficient to keep them submissive and properly respectful of the government."

Surely the kings who ruled Spain in those years were not without their frequent warnings of the dangers which threatened their rule. Their power, however, was to be taken from them at home as well as abroad.

NEWS FROM EUROPE

To the colony in 1808 came the news which set off the movements for independence in South America, the word that Napoleon Bonaparte had extended his war of conquest into Spain and placed his brother, Joseph Bonaparte, on the throne, deposing the Spanish King Charles and imprisoning his heir, Ferdinand VII.

At once the *Cabildo*, or municipal council, presented the viceroy with a memorial stating that in the absence of a king *the sovereignty rested with the people.* Here was the doctrine of people's rights and popular government put into practice. The *Audiencia,* the higher, royalist council, declared as promptly that such an idea was heretical. Thus the line was drawn for the first time between the Church and Crown supporters, who stood for the old ways, and the Americans or Creoles, who stood for the new.

For two years there was confusion in authority, with the Spanish party in control, but the American idea gaining strength. The stage was set for revolution, but when it came the place, the time, and the leader were all unexpected. The revolution began not in the halls of Mexico City, or with the leaders of the State, but in the village of Dolores with a humble priest at its head.

HIDALGO OF MEXICO

HIDALGO OF MEXICO

*"Long live Independence! Long live America! Death
to bad government!"—Grito de Dolores,* 1810.

"THE Father of Mexican Independence," Miguel
Hidalgo y Costilla, was not a young man in the
year 1810, when he sounded the famous *Grito de
Dolores* from the little village where he was priest. Nor
was he the man who had been intended for the leadership of the Creole uprising. A young military officer,
Ignacio Allende, had been destined for that position, but
the plans changed, and it was Allende who made the
famous ride to the home of Hidalgo, and the priest who
marched at the head of the hastily gathered army.

EARLY LIFE

Miguel Hidalgo y Costilla was fifty-seven years old at
this time. Born on May 8, 1753, he was the son of Don
Cristobal Hidalgo y Costilla, and Doña Ana Maria Gal-
laga. That he was of good family is shown not only by
the records of his ancestry on both sides, but also by the
name Hidalgo, a word applied to describe noblemen in
the Spanish tongue, having been contracted from the
phrase *hijo de algo,* which might be translated "son of

somebody." It may have been a comfort to him sometimes to say that name over to himself, for in spite of his good family, he was a Creole, a boy of Spanish blood and pure Spanish ancestry, yet born, as his father and mother had been before him, in this Spanish colony of Mexico. That meant that he was looked down upon, almost as if he had Indian blood in his veins, by the ruling Spaniards from the mother country. It was so in all the colonies of New Spain, from Mexico down through Central America to Venezuela, Peru, and Chile. Bolívar and other future "liberators" were to be humiliated by the same treatment.

Yet Miguel was exceptionally lucky, for while he was still a small boy, some of the restraints were lifted. Creoles were, for the first time since the Conquest, granted the right to go to Mexican colleges and universities, and even to hold offices in the law courts and in the Church, if they were well educated and had sufficient money and influence.

Don Cristobal had four sons, of whom Miguel was the oldest, and he resolved to give them the best education that could be had. The two older boys he destined for the Church, sending them together to a college founded and carried on for more than two hundred years by the Jesuits, at Valladolid, a pleasant town two hundred or more miles west of Mexico City. Notice the name, for this was to be one of the hotbeds of new and progressive political ideas. Today there is a square there called the

"Plaza of the Martyrs," because several patriots were put to death there in the early nineteenth century, and the town has been renamed Morelia in honor of Morelos, Hidalgo's successor. But at this time it was Valladolid, a town with a fine promenade and several beautiful churches and a college, no longer Jesuit, where the Hidalgo boys were being educated.

Miguel learned there the required subjects of that time, Latin, philosophy, and theology, and received his degree of Bachelor of Arts. With that amount of learning he could have gone at once into the priesthood, but this taste of education, within these narrow bounds, had made him eager for more. He and his brother Joaquin went on to the University of Mexico, at Mexico City, for another three years of study, Miguel receiving the further degree of Bachelor of Theology and doing so conspicuously well in his studies that he was called back to teach in his own college at Valladolid.

A MAN OF IDEAS

If it had been only the regular learning of the schools which Miguel Hidalgo had absorbed, he would not have been noticed, except as a brilliant student. But he made himself conspicuous for his independent ideas. He studied subjects not on the list of approved courses, and read books of political theory which were condemned by the Spanish Inquisition, then diligent in persecuting anyone who did not conform to its rigid views of Church and

State. He made contemptuous remarks, too, about his professors, and showed in more ways than one that his was a restless spirit, which did not yield easily to authority. So, though for a few years he held positions of honor and responsibility at the college, becoming an ordained priest during the period, he did not continue as a teacher of young men, but went out in 1785 into parish work. Probably he was becoming too well known for his independent and revolutionary political ideas, as well he might be, for the misgovernment of these provinces by frequently changing Spanish officials was enough to drive any capable young thinker to rebellion. Certainly he was not in favor with the high authorities of Church and State, for in the year 1800, when he was forty-seven years old, he was deprived of the comfortable church and parish over which he was presiding, and denounced to the commissioner of the Inquisition as "unorthodox."

Since the records are all those written by his enemies, who gave him no chance to defend himself, they cannot be taken too seriously. Yet through them comes the picture of the man who, ten years later, was to lead the Mexican Revolution. He was widely read, they said, in French literature, and leaned heavily to French political ideas, which were, of course, utterly opposed to such government as the Spaniards were imposing on their colonies. He had been heard to speak of monarchs as despotic tyrants, and to engage in debate as to whether a republic was not a better form of government than a

MIGUEL HIDALGO Y COSTILLA
1753 - 1811

monarchy. There was the accusation that he was married and had two daughters who lived in his home. Along with this was the tale that he owned a copy of the Koran! Altogether, there was a curiously assorted list of charges, which were evidently not proved, for the case was suspended and the papers put on file, with the comment that one of the accusers was a notorious liar. Still, the case cost Father Hidalgo his comfortable living, and for the next three years he did not have a regular parish but wandered about the provinces of this central portion of Mexico, becoming acquainted with the life of the common people, the Indians and the *mestizos,* with white and Indian blood in their veins.

IN HIS PARISH

Then came the call to Dolores, to succeed his brother Joaquin, who had been curate of the village church and had died. It is here that we may come to know Miguel Hidalgo, not simply as a "hero of independence," standing out above others of his time as a symbol of a popular movement, but as a man among other men, living among Spaniards, Creoles, *mestizos,* and Indians in a typical village and doing what he could to better their conditions. It was a little village, unimportant in the big empire, with its houses clustered about the parish church of *Nuestra Señora de Dolores* (Our Lady of Sorrows). The priest lived in a simple one-story house of a dozen or more rooms, spread out in comfortable Spanish fashion, and therefore, as it proved, ideal for the use to which Hidalgo was to put it. For here he proceeded to set up what we should call, in our day, an industrial and social neighborhood house.

In a way not in the least customary among clergy of that time and region, Father Miguel Hidalgo was interested in his parishioners, the common people of his parish. Like the famous Bartolomé de las Casas, who had been known long before on the Pearl Coast and in Central America as "Protector of the Indians," he sympathized with these long-oppressed natives and set about to help them. The Indians of his parish lived on the neighboring landed estates of the Old Spaniards, not as slaves in a legal sense, but bound to the owners of the land for such labor as was required. While he ministered to them as their priest, Hidalgo began also to plan for their industrial improvement.

He taught them to cultivate the vine [say his biographers] in order that they might learn what wealth was to be obtained from the soil by developing its natural resources. He planted mulberry trees and cultivated the silkworm, that he might in time develop silk manufacture. He taught the Indians the art of tanning hides, and so enabled them to produce leather at a much lower cost than they were accustomed to pay for it when bought of the Spanish merchants. He established a factory in which he introduced better methods of making the earthenware than the Indians had used before the Conquest; and he taught them how to make better bricks than the sun-dried adobes which they had been accustomed to make.

He was enabling them to produce these things for their own benefit, and not for the purpose of enriching some proud and cruel Spaniards. In a few words, he was fitting the Indians of his neighborhood to pursue the occupations of free people rather than those of slaves.

It is a pleasant picture that has come down to us of this village priest among his people: a man of medium height, with stooping shoulders, dark-complexioned, bald, with a fringe of hair that had turned white early, and dressed in the ordinary garb of the curate, a long black cloak or coat, a round sombrero, short trousers, and the usual clerical collar. They were by no means all Indians who came to his house. Hidalgo was intimate with the leading men of the community and region, and with the Spanish landowners, who loaned him money for his industrial experiments and did not press him too hard when he remained deeply in their debt. He held entertainments, even dances, in his community house, which was his home, and there came to them white men and Indians, rich folk and people of the middle and poorer classes.

This would have been enough to get him into trouble, sooner or later, with the authorities, for there were rules issued long since by the House of Trade in Spain that forbade almost everything Hidalgo was doing. There could be no factories in the colonies, lest they compete with the home manufactories. Nothing could be grown which would compete directly with the home market, and the raising of grapes was expressly forbidden, in order to limit the people to Spanish wines. When news of Hidalgo's flourishing industries came to headquarters, officers were sent in all haste to cut down the mulberry trees and root out the grapevines. But they were too late to wipe out the picture and the memory of them from the minds of the Indians. These natives had seen what could be done on this land, and they did not forget it.

Other complaints came to the ears of the officers of the Inquisition. French books of literature, science, and theology were read and discussed by friends who gathered in the curate's hospitable home, and there was a tale that some of Molière's comedies had been translated and acted out of doors in the garden. There was testimony, too, that Hidalgo read every book he could lay hands on, whether it was written in Greek, Latin, French, or Italian, and discussed the contents of them all freely with such as were interested.

ADVOCATE OF INDEPENDENCE

If all Hidalgo's pursuits had been as free from actual threat to Church or State as these, the various charges might have remained on file in the records of the Inquisition. But these were restless, dangerous times in Spain and in the colonies. Napoleon sent his armies through Spain to attack Portugal, and placed his brother Joseph on the Spanish throne, deposing the unpopular, incapable

Charles IV and imprisoning his son, Ferdinand VII.
When the news of these events reached New Spain,
great confusion resulted. The Creoles, who had come
into considerable power during the last part of the former
century, took this chance to declare for freedom, using
as their argument the unwillingness to be ruled by a
foreigner, a Frenchman on the throne of Spain, and
making a great show of loyalty to the imprisoned heir.
The Spaniards, the *gapuchines,* as they were often called
in contempt and anger by the common people, began to
be alarmed by this talk of popular government. There
were mutinies and counter-mutinies in the capital, and
as the power passed from one party to the other and
back again, there grew up a secret movement for complete independence, discussed and organized in secret
societies in many towns and cities.

One of the most active of these groups was the "Literary and Social Club of Querétaro," headed by a Creole
officer who was in command of the local militia. The
province of Querétaro adjoined that of Guanajuato, in
which was located the village of Dolores, and the eager,
restless, intellectual parish priest, Father Hidalgo, was one
of this club's most enthusiastic and prominent members.
Here he could discuss with fellow radicals the French
theories of government by a republic, and share his dis-
content over the mismanagement of the country by the
Spanish officials. While the elected assemblies of the
Government were discussing whether to side with the

Bonaparte group or its opponents, these men in their "Society" were making a plot to seize the control of the country and proclaim independence from Spain.

THE PATRIOT PLAN

It was not a well-thought-out military plan, but only a move to unite all people who wanted freedom. At the fair of San Juan de los Lagos (St. John of the Lakes) on December eighth in this year of 1810, Captain Allende was to proclaim independence and gather under the banner of freedom all those who were secretly eager for this uprising. These leaders, Hidalgo and Allende and the rest, knew how widespread was the readiness for such a move. Hidalgo was only one of many churchmen who were in the movement. It is said that of the local clergy of Mexico four out of every five believed in the political independence of New Spain. The army, officered by many Creoles, had been willingly supporting the Spanish viceroy in defense of the country against the English and against attack by the United States, but they were not interested in Spain's wars in Europe and were talking quietly of a future "Mexico for the Mexicans." It was natural and inevitable that this movement should come out into the open, and this big December gathering of people from many regions seemed an excellent time. At this time the property of Spaniards would be seized, and the government offices taken over.

THE RIDE TO DOLORES

But in September the plot was discovered, as it could hardly help being because of the many who knew of it. A few arrests were made at Queretaro, and orders were given for the arrest of other leaders of the "Literary and Social Club," among them Allende and Hidalgo. There the matter might have ended, for the time being at least, if it had not been for the events of September fifteenth and sixteenth which Mexico remembers.

The governor of the town, Miguel Dominguez, received the order to make the arrests. He was secretly in sympathy with the patriot movement, but was forced by his official position to fulfil the order. His wife, however, Joséfa Maria Ortiz de Dominguez, had no such obligation. She was an ardent patriot, and when she learned of the earlier arrests, she gave a prearranged signal of warning to a village official who lived in the same building, tapping three times on the floor. The man who heard the sound hurried off at once to give the news to Captain Allende, who leaped on his horse and rode the fifty miles to the village of Dolores to inform Hidalgo.

For her part in spreading the alarm Doña Ortiz was soon imprisoned in a convent, while her husband was placed in confinement elsewhere. But both survived the revolution, and she has been honored ever since by the Mexican people as the "heroine of Independence."

Shortly before midnight Allende, with two other leaders of the planned revolt, arrived at the quiet little town of Dolores, where the people were sleeping peacefully in their beds with no knowledge of the happenings elsewhere. The three men wakened the middle-aged curate and told him that several of their number were already in the hands of the authorities.

"Senor Cura," declared one of them, "we are caught in a trap. No human power can save us."

The priest thought for a moment and then seemed to agree.

"I see that we are lost," he said slowly, and then added, "and so no other course remains but for us to go out and seize the *gapuchines.*"

Before the clock struck the hour of midnight, Father Hidalgo went to his church tower and rang the bell. A few men, Indians and others, gathered and were told what had happened. They went at once, with such weapons as they could get in their haste, to the public prison and freed political prisoners held there, telling them that they could have their liberty if they would join the revolt. Next the crowd went to the local barracks, where was stationed a company of Captain Allende's men who gladly joined the company. Before dawn the homes of the leading Spaniards had been entered, and their owners arrested. The town of Dolores was in the hands of the revolutionists, although no violence had been done.

THE "GRITO"

This was a Saturday night, and on Sunday morning, the sixteenth, at five o'clock, Father Hidalgo gathered his strange company in the courtyard of the parish church, and after celebrating Mass spoke to them of the evils of the government by which they were oppressed and the gains which would come to them under a popular rule.

To the listening Indians he said: "My children, this day comes to us a new way of life. Are you ready to receive it? Will you be free? Will you make the effort to recover from the hated Spaniards the lands stolen from your forefathers three hundred years ago?"

The crowd listened with rising enthusiasm and answered his words with a shout.

"Viva Independencia! Viva America! Muera el mal gobierno!" (Long live Independence! Long live America! Death to bad government!)

This was the cry which was to echo through all Mexico and be repeated down the years, the famous *Grito de Dolores*. Such a *Grito* or "Cry" meant, by the Spanish custom, the proclamation by "voice-vote" of the revolution.

Other words were to be added to the *Grito* that day. The little marching army set out on the road that morning, and as they marched, others joined them. As they passed through one town in which was a tiny church with a banner of the Virgin of Guadalupe, patron saint of the Indians, either Hidalgo or one of his curates took the banner from the church and fastened it to one of the soldiers' pikes. With this banner carried at the head of the line, the march continued.

Hidalgo knew his Indians. This was what would make the appeal to them. Every Indian knew the story of the Virgin's appearing as an Indian maiden to a humble laborer in the field in the year 1531, but for us it must be repeated. We tell it in the words of an English military man, Captain Lyon, who printed in London in 1828 his "Journal of a Residence and Tour in the Republic of Mexico in the Year 1826." This was the story as it was told to him in Mexico only sixteen years after the *Grito*.

LEGEND OF GUADALUPE

"Soon after the Conquest," reads the Journal, "a poor, untutored Indian named Juan Diego, while laboring near the foot of the rock Tepeyaca, where the Sanctuary now stands, suddenly heard a peal of music, and saw before him the Blessed Virgin in the attitude and habiliments of the present picture. The man was very naturally astonished; but more so when the Virgin commanded him to go to the bishop of Mexico, and desire him to build a chapel to her honor on that very spot.

"The bishop . . . would not believe in heavenly apparitions; he therefore reproved poor Juan Diego for his credulity, and sent him away. Again the Blessed Virgin appeared, and delivered a more positive command. But the bishop once more dismissed the messenger, with threats of punishment. . . . The mortified Juan Diego again retired to the rock Tepeyaca, where for the third time he tremblingly saw Our Lady, who with some displeasure repeated her orders; to which the man replied by begging a sign for the unbelieving bishop. 'Go,' said the Blessed Mother of God, 'and climb the rock, and on its hitherto barren summit you will find a token. Take it to the bishop, and he will believe.'

"Juan obeyed; and although it was in the depth of winter, he found the once desolate spot covered with the most exquisite flowers in full bloom. Filling therefore his *serape,* or wrapper, with the miraculous roses, he posted joyously to the bishop, who called a number of priests to witness the opening of the *serape;*—when, lo! as the flowers fell from it to the ground, this identical picture [of the Virgin] which I saw was found imprinted on it. . . . Nothing more was now required to enforce conviction. A splendid church was erected and endowed to the Patroness of Mexico; immense wealth was offered at her altar; and from that time every part of New Spain sent, and still does send her, annual tribute; and there is no town of note which has not a church open as a sanctuary for all criminals, and dedicated to Our Lady of Guadalupe."

It was from one of these churches that the banner was taken on that hasty march, and every Indian who joined the procession believed the legend. The woes of three hundred years of oppression, with always the hope for divine aid, were now united in the words added to the *Grito, "Viva Nuestra Senora de Guadalupe!"* ("Long Live Our Lady of Guadalupe!")

To this was added another phrase, long in the minds of many of the revolutionists and quickly picked up by the marching hordes, *"Muera los Gapuchines!"* ("Death to the Spaniards!") That was the cry that had been raised in that revolt of Creoles in the year 1799, and had been heard by the wise viceroy with deep concern. From this hour the movement became a social revolution. The Indians hated the men of the white race who ruled them and forced them to labor. Hidalgo had started a religious and social crusade which was to get beyond his control. Yet he knew that he needed the dark-skinned natives if he and his fellow patriots were to win their battle for independence.

THE WAR

The horrors of the war that followed have been often told. The inhabitants of one region after another joined the insurgents, Creoles as well as Indians flocking to the newly raised standard. One of the important towns was captured, and after that the army was organized, with Hidalgo as captain-general, Allende as lieutenant-general, and the others with lesser titles. On the twenty-third of September this untrained army came to the gates of the city of Guanajuato, in a beautiful valley among mountains rich in silver mines. A successful assault was made on the unprepared city, whose Spanish inhabitants had gathered for defense in a great public granary, recently built. The insurgents fired this building and then massacred those within. Treasure stored there and elsewhere was seized, and the town was looted, with horrible destruction. A few days later Hidalgo took the nearby city of Valladolid, which did not resist lest it suffer the same fate.

Success and plunder attracted more hordes of men, till Hidalgo and his officers had from forty to sixty thousand men to handle and attempt to form into a disciplined army. The task was beyond any human power, within the space of time that the insurgent leaders could gain before the Spanish armies could rally and come against them. Moreover, as one victory followed another, the Creoles became alarmed. If this was to become a race war, they were more closely bound with the Spaniards than with these hordes of Indians.

It was probably because Hidalgo himself feared the excesses which he could not prevent that he did not push forward on Mexico City when he was within easy reach of it. With that capital in such danger that the inhabitants were in panic, he failed to cover the leagues between and throw his troops around it. Allende and other military leaders protested, but the moment passed, and Hidalgo retired to Guadalajara and there tried to set up a form of civil government. With the revolt spreading through the provinces, he evidently felt that there must be some declaration and some plan for the future.

HIDALGO'S PROGRAM FOR MEXICO

His goal, he said, was an elected Congress which should govern Mexico. He also sought the betterment of the condition of his Indians, abolishing the Indian tribute. He proclaimed the liberation of all slaves, and opened the jails to let out political prisoners. Always he maintained that he was fighting the Spanish system, both in Church and State, and not the Church of which he had been a priest. In a series of papers which he published and distributed, he set forth his views and defended the acts which had made the Church excommunicate him. It was a social program which he presented, of crafts encouraged, industry restored, and the "rich products of the fertile land used freely for the good of all the people."

THE BEGINNING OF THE END

Meanwhile the warfare went on, with massacres of prisoners and citizens whenever either one of the opposing forces captured a town. In the midst of all this horror, it is no wonder that many Creoles fought with Spaniards against the revolutionists. His own officers, chief among them Allende, tried to change Hidalgo's military policy, but he was impetuous and determined. Against all advice he insisted, early in January, on confronting Calleja's well-disciplined troops at the bridge of Calderon, outside Guadalajara, with his enormous hordes of Indians. His men held their own bravely until an ammunition wagon at their own rear caught fire, and the flames spread through dried grass and choked and blinded them. After this defeat the officers of the army insisted that Hidalgo give up his command of the troops and retain only his political leadership. They would have done better if they had made this insistence long before, for Hidalgo was no military man. Now their army was scattered; the Indians were deserting, and it was too late.

Allende, who had been given the leadership, determined to abandon central Mexico, and seek help in the United States for the forces which he could unite in northern Mexico. With a thousand men, fourteen coaches, and such money as they could salvage, the leaders started on their dangerous journey. But their plans were betrayed, and as they traversed a desert region, they were attacked and Hidalgo, Allende, and other leaders were captured.

The six-hundred-mile journey back was almost too much for the elderly Hidalgo. In chains and under military guard, they made the forced march across the desert to Chihuahua, where he arrived sadly broken in health, though strong of spirit. Allende and the other military leaders were sentenced by the army court and promptly shot. But Hidalgo had first to be degraded from the priesthood by an elaborate ceremonial, before he could come before the military tribunal to answer the charge of treason to the viceroy and the throne.

During the quiet months of imprisonment, he spent the hours reviewing the strange events of the year, and wrote a "message to all the world," which was his "apology" for all the violence and bloodshed. The Spanish Government showed this paper after his death, and there has been discussion as to whether it is genuine. If it is, it shows that he came back in those weeks to the shelter of the Church, which he had served in peace for so many years, and saw the insurrection as a failure, with a fear that Mexico was not ready for independence as the result would be either dictatorship or anarchy. The years were to prove that he foresaw the dangers all too clearly.

Having thus made his personal peace with God, his Church, and his fellow men, Hidalgo came to his trial with calm and answered the questions put to him with firmness and dignity. There was even a show of spirit when he was asked by what right he had rebelled against the Government, and said loudly and clearly, for all to hear, "With the right which every citizen has when he believes his country is in danger of being lost." When, on July 30, 1811, he was taken out to be executed, he prayed with his last breath that Heaven would favor the struggles of his people and grant them the blessings of Independence. There was no withdrawal from his dedication to that ideal.

"FATHER OF INDEPENDENCE"

Hidalgo has come to stand in the minds of his people as the symbol of patriotism. Indeed, the legends which have gathered about his name in a hundred and more years make it difficult to get back to the simple story of the man of his time, who shared in the violence of the revolution, but went far beyond the fighting in his ideals. In the painting of Mexico's history on the wall of the National Palace stairway, Diego Rivera has put him in the center, with the other figures grouped above, below, and around him. There he stands with broken chains in his hands, and the forbidden mulberry plant and grape-vine at his feet, all three recalling his efforts to help his fellow men, no matter what their race or class. His remains were brought in 1821 to the cathedral of Mexico City, and each September, on the anniversary of the *Grito de Dolores,* while the President of the Republic is ringing the old church bell in the government house, the great Cathedral is brilliantly lighted. So Church and State unite to do him honor. In Dolores itself, now renamed Dolores Hidalgo, a national boulevard leads to the church where he sounded the call for freedom.

MORELOS OF MEXICO

MORELOS OF MEXICO

"My life is of little consequence if only Congress is saved."—Morelos.

SOMETIMES it takes a hundred years for a man to be appreciated. So it has been in Mexico with José Maria Morelos, who took up the work of Hidalgo when that leader dropped it, and carried it on for another four years.

Morelos has always been remembered as a military leader, the chief military genius of the days of revolution in Mexico. That skill was recognized even beyond the bounds of his own country during his own lifetime. "With three such men as Morelos I could conquer the world," said Napoleon Bonaparte as he read of the Mexican guerilla leader's brilliant campaigns.

Only in the twentieth century, however, have the leaders of Mexico begun to realize that in their efforts for reform of their social order they were walking along the path which Morelos had marked out between 1810 and 1815. The troublesome land question, the relation of Church and State, the Indian needs, were all faced and thought through by this man, and in his proposed constitution for Mexico he indicated a wise solution for every problem. If his plans could have been carried out, Mexico would have been saved many years of misery; but he was too far ahead of his times.

AN AMBITIOUS YOUTH

Even in his boyhood José Morelos showed both resolution and ambition. He was born on September 30, 1765, the son of a carpenter, Manuel Morelos of Valladolid, and Juaña Pavon, who was the daughter of a schoolmaster. Perhaps it was the memory of that schoolmaster which gave him courage to seek an education. At any rate, at the opening of the term at the College of San Nicolas in 1790, there appeared this young man of the town, a short, thick-set youth with a round face, a high forehead that showed intelligence, and dark eyes that were steady as they met those of his questioners. He was much older than the boys of the Spanish and Creole families of the town and from the *haciendas* who were coming to be enrolled, and he made no secret of his poverty, or of his humble origin. His parents had always been poor, and after his father's death he had had to give up his schooling and go to work for his Uncle Philip, who was connected with a large *hacienda* and owned also a mule train which went back and forth between Mexico City and the Pacific port of Acapulco, doing much business.

The young man would naturally have continued in this work. The class system of Mexico under colonial rule did not encourage any youth to change his calling or attempt to rise in the world. But José Morelos had always wanted to continue his studies and become a priest, and here he was, at the age of twenty-five, giving up his poorly paid job and seeking admittance with boys of fifteen and sixteen and seventeen. The officials took him in as an undergraduate, letting him attend classes and work his way as best he could. That proved to be a hard way. He was half starved during those college years. But he had his reward. He sat in the philosophy classes of the brilliant young professor of philosophy and theology, Hidalgo y Costilla, and became his friend.

VALLADOLID, CITY OF PATRIOTS

It is interesting to get a picture from our British traveler, Captain Lyon, of this town where these two patriots spent so much time. The moments in the lives of these men on which we of a later time dwell are those of war, but these were balanced by long years of quiet study and teaching. Valladolid pleased the Britisher more than any other town he visited. As he entered it, he was impressed by the "width and airy appearance of its streets, the goodness of the houses, and its magnificent cathedral." He tells of the Alameda, a straight, broad walk on the eastern side of the town, paved with flat slabs and bounded on either edge by low stone walls and benches, overshadowed by rows of fine trees, whose branches frequently joined in the center. By its side ran a road of sufficient width for two carriages, which branched off, about a mile southward, into shady lanes and drives.

The city had but one principal street, but this was broad and clean and cheerful. "The Plaza is remarkable," he says, "as having broad piazzas on three of its sides, and the fine cathedral isolated from all other buildings bounding it on the east. A crowded market is held here, and the venders display their goods, as is the general custom, beneath the shade of rude mat umbrellas. Fruits and vegetables are tolerably abundant; and amongst other luxuries, the *pescado blanco* (or whitefish) is brought from the lake of Pascuaro. The night market on the Sunday is extremely pretty; each little shop having a bright blazing pile of the fragrant Ocote (red pine) in its front, so that from an elevated window the scene is very lively and peculiar. All the houses of Valladolid have flat roofs, the same as in Old Spain, with long waterspouts projecting most incommodiously over the streets. On many of the terraces a fine crop of grasses and mosses was flourishing so luxuriantly that I am astonished at the natives not having taken so good a hint for making little gardens on their roofs, which would give a fresh and lively appearance to the city."

On these shady walks outside the city the patriots walked and talked. They worshipped in the cathedral, one of the most beautiful in the country. This was the city from which the Bishop of Michoacan (the province of which it was the capital) had sent his warning to

JOSÉ MARIA MORELOS
1765 - 1824
He holds the famous Declaration of Independence (1813).

King Charles that the condition of the Indians must be improved if trouble was to be avoided. Ten short years were to prove his words too true.

THE CALL TO WAR

Morelos won his way through to the priesthood, as was his long-time ambition, and after completing his course at San Nicolas served for some fifteen years in different parishes, being simply one more local curate, a humble member of the large company of priests who did faithful service in their churches in the towns and villages of Mexico. But these were troubled times, and no man of Morelos's ability and training could fail to watch the growing unrest of the people under the bad government of the Spanish officials of both Church and State.

Then came September, 1810, with its *Grito de Dolores* sounded out by Father Hidalgo, and in October, as Hidalgo and his growing army marched across the country, Morelos left his church and offered his services to his beloved teacher and to the cause. They were accepted, and in the unbelievable method, or lack of it, of that extraordinary movement, Hidalgo dispatched him with instructions to carry the revolution into the region south of Mexico City and take possession of the well-fortified port of Acapulco—and gave him twenty-five men for the task!

But Morelos had the gift of winning men to his assistance. Within a few months he had attracted several able leaders to whom he gave positions of responsibility, and shortly he had an army, well organized in contrast to most of the other forces in the field. There were three thousand men under him, and he was winning victories for the Independent cause.

AS MILITARY LEADER

The Spaniards hoped to make an end of the rebellion by putting to death, in the summer of 1811, its leaders. After the execution of Hidalgo, and Captain Allende and his brave companions, they rounded up and shot at least thirty more of the Independent chieftains. But Mexico was too big for them, and the fire of revolution which the patriot priest had kindled was smouldering in too many valleys and provinces. Morelos was the strongest of the surviving leaders, and had by the end of that year an army of nine thousand men, fairly well equipped with the arms and supplies which had been captured in his victorious engagements. With this army he began to threaten Mexico City itself, cutting off its supplies on the roads from the south. General Calleja, the extremely able Spanish general, returned from the north, where he had been pursuing other guerilla chiefs, and prepared to meet this southern army.

The Spanish forces were too large for Morelos to venture to meet them in open battle, and in the course of the campaign he and a portion of his army, some three thousand men, were caught in the town of Cuautla, where

General Calleja with his well-trained regiments, number-
ing twelve thousand men, proceeded to attack them. The
attack was repulsed, and after more than one unsuccessful attempt the General settled down, on the nineteenth
of February, 1812, to besiege the town, expecting a speedy
surrender. But the weeks went by, and though he knew
that the men inside the town must be starving, they held
out. The condition of these besieged men was, indeed,
desperate. They were eating the bark of trees, and soap,
and the flesh of every living creature within the town,
however repulsive it was. But the rainy season was due,
and they were hoping that, with its coming, General
Calleja's troops, unused to life in the tropics, would be
weakened by sickness. But the rainy season was delayed
far beyond its usual time. Daily Morelos and his fellow
officers looked at cloudless skies and hoped and prayed
for rain that did not come.

The time came when something must be done. They
could hold out no longer. Then Morelos carried through
one of the most brilliant exploits of his career. Under
cover of night on the second of May, his soldiers in three
divisions stole out quietly, stealthily, for two hours from
midnight on, overpowering the sentries so that it was
some time before the Spaniards discovered what was happening. When the firing of the sentries finally roused
the army, the Independents had reached a deep gorge
beyond the Spanish lines, and were on the edge of open
country. In the first confusion Spanish troops began to

fire on one another, thinking each moving column was of the enemy. Meanwhile, at a signal previously agreed upon, Morelos's troops scattered far and wide.

When they finally met at the appointed place, only seventeen men were missing. After his ten weeks of siege, General Calleja captured only an empty town, empty save for such women and children as had been necessarily left behind, whom he had put to death. The General returned to Mexico City announcing that he had taken Cuautla and claiming a triumph. But the story of the escape of the Independent army had reached there before him, and the people of the town knew better.

In a comedy presented in a theater a day or two later, an actor who was taking the part of a soldier was made to say to his superior officer, "Here is the turban of the Moor whom I took prisoner." The General then inquired, "And where is the prisoner?" "He escaped," replied the soldier; and the audience roared with laughter.

During his first year Morelos had fought twenty-six engagements and won all but two of them. From now on he and his army swept on through southern Mexico until he was master of most of the region. It was this series of successes which won for him the admiration of Napoleon Bonaparte, and gave him his place as one of the chief military heroes of Mexico's wars. It was, on both sides, a severe and bloody war. But wherever he went, Morelos enforced in the regions which he occupied a rough-and-ready justice, collecting taxes in orderly fashion, putting local men in charge of the districts, and punishing by death any of his soldiers convicted of looting.

A CONGRESS CALLED

But military victory was not his end or aim; nor did he seek dictatorship. When, after this second year of fighting, he had won in August of 1813 his long-anticipated capture of the strategic fort of Acapulco, that fortress which he had been sent to take in the first month of the revolution under Hidalgo, he felt himself in a position to carry out his plans for the future conduct of the war and the government of the nation. He recognized that the revolution was still too much a set of separate efforts, with too many leaders, both north and south, and too little unity. He therefore called a Congress, which was to meet in Chilpancingo in September. The provinces which he had freed from Spanish rule were to elect their delegates; for those not yet freed he himself appointed representatives.

It was a small body which met; a committee, we should say, rather than a Congress. There were only eight men, five from the insurgent provinces already successful, and three from those still occupied by Calleja's men. Within a year the number was to increase to forty. But this little group, with their clear-thinking leader, issued the Declaration of Independence of November 6, 1813, the first Declaration of Independence of Mexico. In this famous document, with the Constitution proclaimed a year later, we see the mind of Morelos, or, indeed, as one of his Mexican biographers has said, his soul. These ideals, and his devotion to them, even to the sacrifice of his life, won for Morelos his place among Mexico's Immortals. Here is the leader who has been called the "greatest thinker whom the whole Independent movement produced," the man whose program is quoted by Mexican Liberals to this day.

All over Latin America, from Mexico to Central America and south to Chile and Argentina, revolutionary movements began under cover of a cautious statement of allegiance to the imprisoned king of Spain, Ferdinand VII, heir to the throne, who was kept from it by the ruling Bonapartes of France. Hidalgo had made such a pronouncement. The Congress of Chilpancingo, under Morelos's leadership, and with only one dissenting voice, cut through this pretence.

THE MEXICAN DECLARATION

"Owing to present conditions in Europe," it asserted, the "exercise of its usurped sovereignty" had been recovered by Anahuac (an Aztec name which it adopted for Mexico), and its dependence on the Spanish throne was forever broken and dissolved. Congress, an American Congress, chosen by the people, was competent to establish laws for the best government and happiness of the people.

The Declaration stated that it professed and recognized no other religion than the Catholic, and that the government would protect it with all its power. Thus it an-

swered the charge that the revolution was against the
Church. But in the program of the future, as stated in
both documents, the Declaration of November 6, 1813,
and the Constitution proclaimed a year later, the Church
was to be supported by voluntary contributions, with the
system of enforced taxation and tribute done away. Here
was the beginning of the separation of Church and State
on the political side.

Under the colonial system which still existed where
Spain ruled, there had been endless distinctions of caste
and race, as none knew better than this leader who had
worked on a *hacienda* until he was twenty-five years old,
and then experienced the difficulties of a poor student and
a poor curate in small parishes. These barriers must be
abolished, as a part of the establishment of the sovereignty
of all the people.

"Sovereignty emanates directly from the people," asserted the Declaration. "Laws must extend to all alike,
without exceptions or privileges. As a good law is above
all men, those laws which our Congress shall enact must
be such as to compel obedience and patriotism, to moderate both extreme wealth and poverty, and so to increase
the wages of the poor that they may improve their habits
and do away with ignorance, violence, and theft."

A SOCIAL PROGRAM

Here was a forecast of the social legislation which was
part of Morelos's program. He saw that the huge landed
estates, with their system of servitude for the people work-

ing on them, must be broken up and distributed,—a solution of the land problem which has been the goal of Mexican Liberals in the present century as it was for this prophetic leader. "The effective pursuit of agriculture," he wisely said, "consists in having many individuals devote themselves to the cultivation of small areas." So he announced the confiscation of the enormous land holdings of the Spanish Church, as well as of the rich aristocrats, and their division, half for the carrying on of the expenses of the government, and half for distribution according to his plan of small plots of ground for the poorer classes. Morelos was a good Catholic himself, going always to confession before he entered battle and giving respect to the Church which he had served as curate. But he was able to see the Church as apart from the great feudal organization of three hundred years of Spanish occupation, and was as eager to free it and make it truly national as should be the other institutions of the country.

There were lesser matters to be regulated, and for all these the two documents showed a liberal and advanced position. The conduct of the war was to be reformed, giving regard for the treatment of prisoners and for the protection of people in conquered towns. There were orders for the fair treatment of Europeans who might choose to remain in the country. For the carrying out of these and all other measures there was to be the new government to be set up by the Congress and exercising the

A VILLAGE CHURCH IN MEXICO

Around the church and the school which was often next door to
it, centered the life of the common people.

usual executive, legislative, and judicial functions. Morelos's goal was a ruling Congress, and for this goal he sacrificed too much.

"SERVANT OF THE NATION"

It is to his honor that he refused all titles for himself as executive save that of "Servant of the Nation," declining to be addressed as "His Highness." It is eternally to his credit that he went through the whole undertaking without a suspicion of his having taken a single penny for himself, although huge sums passed through his hands. But he made the mistake, most unusual among leaders of the Spanish American forces, of not reserving for himself sufficient power. By the terms of the constitution there was to be a threefold leadership, instead of a single president. Parliamentary government was an excellent goal, but to divide leadership at this time among three men and to shift the control in the midst of the war and give it into the hands of an inexperienced Congress was a serious mistake, as events proved.

Meanwhile, orders had come from Spain deposing the viceroy of Mexico and placing General Calleja in that office. Now the Spaniard could turn all the forces of the country to subdue the revolution. In a bold move he armed all Creoles who would fight on his side, thus lining up under his standard not only the Spanish aristocracy but the middle-class men of Spanish descent who had come in these weary years to desire peace for their war-torn country, whether it came under Spain or any other strong leadership. From this time on Morelos was fighting an unequal battle against too heavy odds. It was a civil war, not a clear-cut contest for freedom.

MORELOS AND ITURBIDE

At the end of the year 1813, the year of the Declaration of Independence, there came the first serious setback for Morelos, a military incident remembered because it put over against each other two Mexican leaders who had different ideals, Morelos and Iturbide. Morelos had marched north to capture his birthplace, Valladolid, famous seat of liberty, which was his choice for the location of his new parliamentary government. But a young colonel, Agustín de Iturbide, was in charge of the Spanish forces there. This man had known Hidalgo in the earlier days, but had chosen to throw in his lot against the revolutionists. He had gained a reputation as an able fighter and a cruel conqueror.

By a slip in judgment unusual for him Morelos failed to defend adequately his position on a rocky height outside the city, thinking himself and his men sufficiently protected for a night by the difficulty of scaling the rocks. Iturbide succeeded in surprising him there, and in the fighting and escape the Independent army was scattered. From that day the tide of the war turned. There were Independent victories, but the defeats were more numerous. It was in the fall of that year, 1814, that the Congress

—: 52 :—

met and proclaimed the new Constitution. But they were
forced to move from place to place for their deliberations,
as one stronghold after another which Morelos had won
was retaken by the royalist forces.

This Congress lost confidence in their leader, as he suffered defeats. They appointed a committee of their number to carry on the war, and Morelos took their decision
without protest, declaring that he was ready to fight as
a private in the ranks if Congress so decided. Perhaps the
cause was lost already, but without his personal magne-
tism and brilliant leadership there was no chance. The
chiefs who took charge in the different provinces disagreed with one another, and divided their forces un-
wisely, while Iturbide fought on with terrific attacks, cap-
turing one chieftain after another.

"SAVE THE CONGRESS"

In the end it was for the protection of this Congress that
Morelos sacrificed his own safety. They had moved from
place to place, and at last decided that they must go over
the mountains to Tehuacan, in the province of Puebla, to
establish a new seat of government where they would be
safe. But the journey was through a region occupied by
Spanish forces, and would be not only long but perilous.
They turned to Morelos, asking him to conduct them, and
without hesitation he consented. He endeavored to make
arrangements to meet another Independent general mid-
way in the journey, but his messengers were intercepted.

Instead of meeting the supporting troops which he had expected, he found himself attacked by the enemy, which had learned of his plans. Morelos had only a small force of five hundred men. As soon as he saw the danger, he ordered one of his officers to take the main body of this army and continue to escort the fleeing Congress to a place of safety, while he himself with only fifty men endeavored to divert the attention of the enemy and make them think that they were attacking the entire force.

The strategy was successful. The Congress got through safely. But Morelos was captured. He would not have had it otherwise. Government by a representative body of citizens had been his ideal, and it is said that he had danced with joy when the Constitution was adopted in the previous autumn and this Congress installed. When he made the final decision for their safe-conduct, he declared this faith.

"My life is of little consequence," he said to those who protested the plan, "if only Congress is saved. My career was run when I saw an Independent government established."

He made another bold speech on that day of his capture. The Spanish officers who had taken him asked him what he would have done with them if the victory was his, and he said promptly: "I would have given you two hours to prepare for death, and then I would have shot you."

They gave him much more than two hours. They took him to the capital in chains, and all along the way the people came out to have a sight of this famous rebel leader, who had come so near to victory. The viceroy had restored the Holy Office, obeying the command of a reactionary government in Spain. So Morelos had to go before this Church tribunal and be degraded from the priesthood, as Hidalgo had been, before he could be shot by the military men. It was a testimony to his importance that five hundred of the leading personages of the city gathered to see that ceremonial.

The viceroy was warned by the popular sympathy for the prisoner not to have the execution take place within the city. It is said that even his jailer offered to let him go free, but Morelos refused, knowing that the man could not escape punishment if he was suspected. To avoid any hostile demonstration they took him to a village a few miles away, and there he was shot on December 22, 1815.

Two comments made by historians sum up his service to the cause of independence. "With him," says one, "ended the heroic days of the Mexican Revolution." The other adds, "Morelos had carried the Revolution to the point where failure of the movement for independence was impossible." Mexicans of today say that if the social reforms he advocated could have been enacted, the nation would have been spared many of the trials of the hundred years that followed his death.

ITURBIDE, SOLDIER AND EMPEROR

ITURBIDE, SOLDIER AND EMPEROR

*"The love of my country led me on to Iguala; it
was my stepping-stone to the throne."*—Iturbide.

HERE is a man whose life stands over against the
careers of Hidalgo and Morelos in as sharp contrast as black against white. Yet it belongs in the picture,
for he was the Mexican leader in whose brief rule the
political tie which bound Mexico to Spain was cut, a man
whom his countrymen did hail as "Liberator" for a time
until he became "Emperor" through the ambition which
led to his downfall. It is an interesting career, a disturbing one, for at times it came so near to greatness.

BEFORE THE REVOLUTION

Agustín de Iturbide was proud of his family. He says
of himself at the time when the *Grito de Dolores* was
sounded: "I was . . . taking care of my estates and living independently; nor did I trouble myself about obtaining public situations, of which I did not stand in need,
either as a means of subsistence, or as an honor to my
name, since Providence had given me an illustrious origin." He was twenty-seven years old at that time, having
been born at Valladolid, that center of free political dis-

cussion, on September 27, 1783, his father, José Joaquin de Iturbide, being a Spaniard, and his mother, Maria Joséfa Aramburu, a Mexican. He always claimed that he was Creole, but there seems little doubt that he was really a *mestizo,* with Indian blood in his veins. Such a distinction would have mattered little save in the caste-ridden colony. But the Spaniards who had been born overseas kept all the higher offices, so that Creole young men, though of pure Spanish descent, had no chance for advancement. There was always a bitterness among these young natives, which could be turned easily to rebellion. But there was also likely to be a feeling of superiority over *mestizos* and Indians. When it came, in Hidalgo's time, to a choice between siding with Spaniards or with the lower classes, many Creoles chose the Spanish-led side.

Agustín had shown no distinction in his boyhood. He made no effort to acquire the education which Morelos sought so eagerly in the same town, but avoided school as much as he could. At sixteen he entered the provincial militia, serving without pay as was the custom among the militiamen at that time. When he was twenty-two he married into one of the well-known families of the city, and five years later, in 1810, was living a comfortable life, helping his father in the care of the family *haciendas,* when he was approached by young men who were plotting against the government. He was a lieutenant in the militia by that time.

His response to the movement for independence is interesting, for it was the usual feeling of the well-to-do, conservative people, both clergy and landowners. He tells it himself in a personal sketch of his life written while he was in exile in 1823.

> In the year 1810. . . . the revolution, projected by Don Miguel Hidalgo, curate of the town of Dolores, burst forth; and this chieftain offered me a Lieutenant-general's command. The offer was certainly a tempting one to a young man devoid of experience, and at an age to be led away by ambitious pursuits. I nevertheless rejected it, because I was of the opinion that the curate's plans were badly conceived, and could not fail to produce disorders, blood, and destruction, without ever attaining the real object in view.
>
> Time proved the truth of my predictions.

Iturbide always wanted it understood that he was not disloyal to the interests of his native country in the years when he fought with the viceroy's troops. "If I myself, at that period, took up arms, it was not to make war on the Americans," he wrote later; "but rather to put down the lawless bands by which the country was infested."

OFFICER IN THE SPANISH ARMY

In the years that followed he proved himself an able officer, winning victories against several of the guerilla chiefs, and especially against Morelos in the last year of the patriot's life. Probably as a reward, he was put by the Spaniards in charge of one of the big military districts. But the cruelty and harsh rule which had been conspicuous in his dealings with conquered enemies, made him unpopular among the people of the region, and he undertook, too, to turn the office to his own profit. One of his official duties was to provide troops for safe-conduct to silver trains, moving from the rich mines of the district to the main route of travel. Iturbide proceeded to exact a percentage of the silver being transported, in return for protection from the rebels or from robbers.

The protests of the mineowners came to the officials in the capital, and Iturbide was summoned to answer their charges. The court never pronounced against him, and the case was put on file with no statement of guilt. But it was thought unwise to keep him in official positions, and he found himself out of active duty in the army. Whether in genuine love of the Church, or penitence for misdoings, he retired to a convent, where he lived for a considerable time. However, the place he selected was frequented by leading government officials as well as clergy. The attractive and personable officer was soon intimate with many of these men.

SEPARATION FOR MEXICO

In these years there were important happenings in Spain, which were to lead almost inevitably to the separation of the colonies from the weakened kingdom. These events made quick shifts take place in Mexico City and the region for which it was capital. In Hidalgo's time there had come the liberal Constitution of 1812, issued by a *junta* which was governing for the imprisoned King Ferdinand VII, while the French Bonapartes claimed and occupied the throne. Its provisions had given the colonies a taste of liberal government, with the Inquisition withdrawn, freedom of the press announced, and the declaration that church property was to be confiscated. Then, in 1814, the king had regained his throne and abolished that Constitution, replacing it by a thoroughly reactionary series of orders and rules. Naturally the upper-class Mexicans did not enjoy having the rights which they had enjoyed so abruptly snatched away. King Ferdinand was playing unintentionally into the hands of those who desired independence from Spain by making his rule so obnoxious.

Revolution came first in the mother country. In 1820 the Liberals of Spain forced the king to restore the Constitution of 1812 and establish for the time being a Liberal rule, which should extend to the colonies. But that was not what the ruling powers in Mexico desired. They wanted independence of Mexico in so far as it was necessary in order to let them keep things going as they were, without the disturbance of these revolutionary ideas, which seemed to be spreading in Europe and even in South America under Bolívar and other national leaders.

Iturbide described, in his autobiography, the sentiment of the leaders, as he saw it: "The Americans, as a whole, certainly wished independence; but they were not agreed as to the manner in which it was to be attained, or the

form of government that was afterward to be adopted.
. . . Many wished an absolute monarchy—others, a moderate one, with the Spanish constitution as its basis; some, with a new code; whilst, at the same time, there were strenuous partisans for a federate, and others for a central republic."

ITURBIDE AND GUERRERO

A new viceroy, looking about for a Mexican leader who could undertake the pacification of the country, and bring the guerilla uprisings to an end, chose the deposed colonel, of whom clergy and officials spoke well. Iturbide was given command of royalist forces, with which to fight the remaining Independent troops. The chief disturbance was in the south, where one of Morelos's ablest officers, Vicente de Guerrero, had kept up the Independent rebellion. Near the end of the year 1820 Iturbide moved south with his troops, encamping near the insurgent region.

There was reason for concern about Guerrero's power. He was a brilliant general, and had built up a formidable army, with which he intended to threaten the capital. But Iturbide, after a few half-hearted sallies against the rebels, proceeded to open negotiations with them. His desire was to unite his forces with those under the Independent leader. Then the two could start a revolution by which they could throw off the authority of Spain. In this plan he was probably backed by many of his clerical

AGUSTÍN DE ITURBIDE

1783 - 1824

"My country was from a colony transformed into a great
and independent empire."

friends, with whom he had been living. But only an occasional friend, to whom he confided his ideas, had any notion of the plans which were seething in Iturbide's mind, nor of his own vision of himself as the savior, the "Liberator" of his country.

It took him a considerable time to convince Guerrero of his sincerity, but he finally won over that honest, simple-minded, able fighter and leader to his scheme for the immediate independence of Mexico. The two men met in the obscure little village of Iguala, which was to become famous from the "Plan of Iguala," which Iturbide issued there. This plan was to be the basis of the final separation from Spain, which came in its train.

THE PLAN OF IGUALA

A political plan might naturally be dull reading, particularly a century and more after its time. But this "Plan of Iguala" is an exception because we see in it the cleverness and really statesmanlike ability of this man whom we are following. Iturbide had always insisted that he stayed on the royalist side, instead of allying himself with Hidalgo and the later Independents, in the hope, as he once put it, that he could thus serve "the Mexicans, the King of Spain, and the Spaniards." In this plan he tried to combine all three interests, with the Mexican first.

He proclaimed complete independence from Spain, declaring that was the only way to remedy the evils which arose from the great distance from Madrid. The moment had arrived for Europeans living in Mexico, Creoles, and Indians to unite for the common good. "At the head of a determined and valiant army," he declared to his listening troops, "I proclaim the independence of Mexico."

The Catholic religion was to be preserved and protected, with no other religion tolerated. That gave assurance to the clergy, as the first provision gave encouragement to those who had fought for independence.

The third provision guaranteed equal treatment to Spaniards and Creoles, thus protecting the people who feared another revolution like that of Hidalgo, and also giving their due rights to the native-born Creoles.

These were the "Three Guaranties," the *Trigarante,* as they were called, "Independence, Religion, Union." By the power of his personality and enthusiasm Iturbide won his army over to them. In the midst of wild enthusiasm the army, encamped at the little village, swore as one man to uphold the Plan, even to the shedding of blood if need be. The army was to be from that day the *"Trigarante* Army," with a tricolor flag, green standing for Independence, white for Religion, and red for Union.

There were curious "understandings" in connection with this Plan. Mexico was to be independent, yes! But it was to be, not a republic, but a constitutional monarchy, under Ferdinand VII himself, if he chose to leave behind his somewhat uncertain kingdom and rule in the New World; or if he did not, under some other member of the Spanish royal family, or a member of a reigning house in Europe. In a later version Iturbide altered that by adding "or under him whom the *Cortes* for the Empire shall appoint." Iturbide was not the only leader in New Spain who felt that a monarchy was the best method of government, though with a strong parliament. There were those who felt this was best in Central America, and in Peru and other South American countries. The idea that Ferdinand VII might himself come over and start such an American empire seems utterly astonishing, at this distance in time; but the mention of the possibility made the royalists feel that separation from Spain was more safe.

The Plan was sent to the viceroy, who promptly rejected it, as one would expect he would. But it spread like wildfire through the country, and a new viceroy, who came to take his place in midsummer, finally agreed to it, under pressure of Iturbide's marching armies. It was at this time that the change was made which allowed for a monarch chosen by the *Cortes* of the country. On September 27, 1821, the *Trigarante* army entered Mexico City with Iturbide at its head, greeted on this his thirty-eighth birthday as the "father and liberator of his country." There was a gorgeous demonstration, with a gold key of the city presented on a platter of silver.

MEXICO A SOVEREIGN NATION

"Six months sufficed to loosen the knot which had hitherto bound the New and Old World together," wrote Iturbide in his autobiography two years later. "Without bloodshed, conflagrations, robberies, or depredations . . . my country was . . . from a colony transformed into a great and independent empire."

The Mexican *junta* met on the following day and elected Iturbide president, signing at the same time a declaration that Mexico was henceforth a sovereign nation. A regency was soon appointed to serve until an emperor was chosen or arrived, with the new viceroy one of its members, and in a short time this official departed for Spain to carry the report of the events to the court.

Mexico was independent, but it was not the independence for which Hidalgo and Morelos, with their followers, had fought and died. It is sad to read the story of the people's enthusiasm in the light of what was so soon to happen. When Iturbide rode into the city on that September birthday of his, mounted on a black charger and welcomed by the City Council and the Aldermen, he came out on the balcony of the Palace to be greeted by a wildly applauding people, and to witness a grand parade of sixteen thousand soldiers. That was his greatest day in the service of the cause of independence. Then he spoke words that deserved to be remembered.

"Now you know how freedom is won," he said to the listening throngs; "to you falls the task of achieving your own happiness."

It was a difficult task which Iturbide and the Congress faced. After twelve years of warfare the national treasury was empty; there was a big army which expected to be kept on the pay roll, and the commerce of the country and its agricultural life had suffered greatly. There were plots almost at once for changing the government, and in the late spring Iturbide had probably come to the conclusion that he must take over the power, if he was to succeed. Whether by his initiative, or not, the cry was raised one evening by a sergeant among the troops, "Viva Agustín I."

HE BECOMES EMPEROR

The soldiers took up the cry, and a huge mob appeared before the President's dwelling, demanding that he proclaim himself Emperor of Mexico. In his story of that May eighteenth Iturbide represents himself as "astonished and appalled" by the summons, and reluctant to accept the crown thus given him. Only the advice of a friend, who felt that the people would take refusal as an offence, made him agree, he says, to the people's call. The judgment of history is, however, that he had been expecting to be forced into this act, which he desired.

On the following morning, May 19, 1822, Iturbide went by invitation to an extraordinary session of Congress. As he approached the building where it met, the crowds in the streets took the horses from his carriage and drew him to the door. All night there had been the ringing of bells and the firing of cannon, and the people thus summoned swarmed into the hall where the Congress was meeting and demanded that the representatives declare him Emperor. Naturally the Congress passed that vote.

Whatever the Emperor's declared reluctance to take office, from the moment of his choice he threw himself into the game of being a monarch with all his heart. Instead of taking his honors simply, Iturbide set up a court such as would belong only in the most ornate days of European medieval splendor. He gave lengthy titles to many personal officials, appointed gentlemen and ladies of the bedchamber, and members of the Imperial Guard, and even instituted an Order of Knights. The crown was made hereditary, and all his family were declared to be princes and princesses. The coronation in July was an elaborate pageant, which pleased the crowds but disturbed the members of the Independent party, who had fought so long for their country's freedom and for a new, liberal government. The Emperor began to have trouble with his Congress, and the more the difficulties multiplied, the more arbitrary and violent he became.

HIS APPEARANCE

An American, Joel Poinsett, later to be Minister to Mexico, traveled through Mexico during that year, and happened to be in Mexico City on the day when Iturbide suddenly dissolved the Congress which had so annoyed him. He went the following day and saw the Emperor meet a new Congress, watching with true democratic disgust as "His Majesty" entered the hall preceded by a crowd of attendants bearing lights. He also met Iturbide in his own apartments, where he was received with courtesy and entertained for half an hour, finding the Emperor agreeable and with an unembarrassed manner.

He is about five feet ten or eleven inches high, stoutly made and well proportioned. His face is oval, and his features are very good, except his eyes, which were constantly bent on the ground or averted. His hair is brown with red whiskers, and his complexion fair and ruddy, more like that of a German than of a Spaniard.

Disapproval breathes through every sentence of Mr. Poinsett's "Notes" on this man. His exercise of power he characterizes as arbitrary and tyrannical. "With pleasing address and prepossessing exterior, and by lavish profusion, he has attached the officers and soldiers to his person, and so long as he possesses the means of paying and rewarding them, so long will he maintain himself on the throne; when these fail, he will be precipitated from it. . . . To judge from his public papers, I do not think him a man of talents. He is prompt, bold, and decisive, and not scrupulous about the means he employs to obtain his ends."

THE EMPIRE ENDS

During 1821 and 1822 the effort had been made to expand the new empire to include the countries of Central America. That effort was not wholly successful. Nor were Iturbide's frantic attempts to improve the finances of the country by printing paper money. Confusion grew, and new insurgent leaders appeared on the scene and began to agitate for the Emperor's removal. Within less than a year of his being announced emperor, Iturbide had lost his power. He knew it, and sent a message to his old Congress, telling them that he had taken the crown only because he was forced to do so, and that now he desired to abdicate, unwilling to remain unless the people wanted him. He also offered to go into exile.

The Congress accepted his offer, declaring that he had come to the throne by an act of violence. On May 11, 1823, the Emperor with his family and a few friends, sailed for Europe, where he lived quietly for a few months. But he desired to return. Informing the Congress that Spain was seeking to reconquer Mexico, he asked that he might come home and fight for independence. The government, in answer, passed a decree that if he was found on Mexican soil, he was to be shot. Not knowing of this order, he landed on the western coast of the Gulf of Mexico and was recognized, though he was traveling incognito. The legislature of the province decided that the decree of the national Congress should be carried out immediately, and on July 19, 1824, he was shot.

The news of his death shocked Europe, and in Mexico the conservative party protested the act and raised him to the role of hero and martyr. In 1838, under a conservative government, his remains were removed to the cathedral at Mexico City in honor of his services in freeing his country.

DON JOSÉ DEL VALLE

DON JOSÉ DEL VALLE

"His contemporaries called him 'The Wise.'"

IN 1934 there was discovered in the Archives of the Guatemalan Government a precious document which had long been missing. It was the Declaration of Independence of Central America, proclaimed on September 15, 1821, a priceless paper which had been tied up in a package with other papers of the period and overlooked. With the finding of that document, signed by the leading patriots of the five republics now called Central America, there was a fresh interest in the signers whose names were on its final page.

AUTHOR OF THE CENTRAL AMERICAN DECLARATION OF INDEPENDENCE

On the first line was the signature of José Cecilio del Valle, known to be the author of that Declaration. His portrait shows a man so like some of our own "founders" and signers of our Declaration of 1776 that it might be substituted for one of the less familiar paintings in historic Philadelphia or Boston's Faneuil Hall, and no one would find it inappropriate. He looks out from the canvas with a friendly, thoughtful gaze, the lines of gentle humor

—: 75 :—

around his mouth softening the firmness of the chin. It is not surprising that this Honduran was honored with membership in the Academy of Science of Paris, and was an intimate friend of the distinguished British economist, Jeremy Bentham. Such a man was certainly well-fitted to write the Declaration of Independence that is recalled by an annual September Fifteenth Independence Day in each of the mid-continent republics.

THE MAKING OF A SCHOLAR

It is interesting that Central America, then known as the Captaincy of Guatemala, could provide such a man with the education he desired. Outside the cities the life was primitive, with large Indian and *mestizo* populations. But the chief cities were centers of Spanish life, with Old World customs and culture.

José del Valle was born on November 22, 1780, in the town of Choluteca, Honduras. His family moved to Guatemala City when he was nine years old, and he went through the usual courses of study at the university, earning his degrees of Bachelor of Philosophy and Bachelor of Law and being admitted to the bar in 1803. But he had had much besides this formal training. There had been private lessons in a variety of subjects, including rhetoric, algebra, geometry, literature, English, Italian, and French; and he had passed with distinction a public examination at the university in logic, metaphysics, and experimental physics.

JOSÉ CECILIO DEL VALLE
1780 - 1834

It was a broad sweep of studies for a young man of that day. The colonial government could not fail to take notice of so brilliant and personable a young lawyer, and during the next dozen years he held under it several public offices, one being that of Minister of War, another the post of legal adviser to the Tobacco Monopoly, and a third, surprisingly for one who was to have his future, the job of censor of the government's official publication, the only newspaper permitted in the colony, the *Gaceta de Guatemala.* During those years he wrote books on commerce, political economy, and law, but was always regarded, according to the archbishop of that period, as a "model of Spanish loyalty."

In 1820, when the new, liberal, Spanish Constitution gave freedom of the press and wider opportunity for self-government to the colonies, he was ready to take a leading part in discussions of future independence. Two publications began then to appear and be discussed by all the intellectuals, one advocating immediate independence, the other, founded by Valle, declaring that the country was not yet ready. Both periodicals recognized, however, that the time would soon come of separation from the weakened Spanish mother country. Opposing the more radical doctrines of *El Editor Constitucional,* which represented the party led by Delgado, Valle's *Amigo de la Patria* (Friend of the Fatherland) counseled the slower methods in the desire for a sure foundation of unity among the provinces.

THE FIFTEENTH OF SEPTEMBER, 1821

So matters went along till the middle of September, 1821, when northern provinces of the Captaincy were choosing annexation with Mexico under Iturbide, and General Gainza called the meeting to consider what measures must be taken to satisfy the people's excited demands. On the morning of the fifteenth, with eager crowds looking on and listening, Valle made the first important speech, advocating independence as both necessary and just, but advising that, for the sake of future unity, it be not proclaimed until the other sections of the Captaincy (that is, such units as Salvador, Costa Rica, etc.) had formally made their declaration. The Independents, however, pressed for immediate action. It was evident from the applause of the crowds that this was what the people wanted, and Valle and his supporters held back no longer.

It is a curious picture that we have here, unlike that of any other Declaration of Independence of the Americas. Here was Gainza, the representative of the crown, presiding over an assembly of Spanish officials and Creoles, deciding whether the country should separate from the mother country or not. Here was Valle, then Minister of War, but a native, advocating the separation, as were other Church and State officers. Valle was drawing up the paper, which declared the desire of Guatemalans to be free and urged that all citizens of the different regions

—: 78 :—

proceed to choose delegates for a national Congress. Meanwhile the governing power was to rest in the hands of a small advisory *junta,* to which, within twenty-four hours, there were appointed seven other men, among them Valle and another famous jurist, Miguel Larreinaga.

From this time on, says Ramon Rosa, Valle "gave his undivided loyalty to the new order; his whole thought and labor were devoted to the noble purpose of organizing the young Republic, on which he lavished the wealth of his genius."

IN ITURBIDE'S CONGRESS

He was chosen representative of Honduras in this new government, and devoted his strongest efforts to opposing the annexation of Guatemala by Mexico, which Iturbide as emperor was forcibly urging, with Gainza lending his influence to the proposal. When the opposition failed and the new arrangement was made, Valle was chosen one of the representatives in the new Congress of Mexico, where he represented his country with such eloquence and gained such leadership by his ability and his independent ideas that the Emperor would have none of it. With his customary high-handedness, Agustín I, as Iturbide was called, had Valle shut up in prison, where he stayed for some months.

Such treatment of a deputy of his distinction roused protests which led to his sudden release on a February day in 1823 with an appointment as Secretary of Foreign

Affairs for Iturbide's empire, the astonishing offer being, as it was said, in reparation for the wrongs he had suffered in his unjust imprisonment. Valle refused the office, but he could not escape it. A month later he resigned, giving this time personal as well as official reasons. He had worked day and night to keep the parts of the great Empire, including his own Central American provinces, at peace, but his health was suffering. Letters from Honduras declared his return necessary to save himself and his family from financial calamities. He was urgent in his desire to depart while he might still make the long journey, for the condition of the Empire was getting so serious as to make travel dangerous.

Again the Emperor, who had treated him so roughly, insisted that he remain, and in the following weeks this Honduran statesman is credited with having done much to bring about the end of the Empire and the abdication of Iturbide without violence and bloodshed.

With the dethroned Emperor safely out of the country, the Congress met with the new Mexican government. At this session the distinguished member from Guatemala proceeded to present the case of his country, proving the illegality of the annexation which he had so long protested. The protest was heard with respect, and the right of Central America to choose its own form of government was recognized. On July 1, 1823, after his strange experience in Mexico City, Valle could start home with a copy of a decree declaring the independence of Central

America from Mexico. That chapter of American history was ended.

BACK IN CENTRAL AMERICA

While he had stood out against this annexation, Valle had had dreams, even before he went to Mexico, of a larger unity for the Americas. In a paper written February 23, 1822, he expressed the wish that there might convene in some province of Central America a "General Congress of Deputies of America," with the double purpose of "outlining a plan to prevent any province of America from being taken by foreign invaders" and of "forming a federation which would include all the States of America . . . and formulate an economic plan which would enrich them." Thus this far-sighted statesman looked, like Bolívar of South America, into the future of Pan Americanism.

Back in his native land Valle played an important part in the framing of the Constitution, but lost once and again, by close party votes and factional disputes, the election to the office of president. It was always easy for him to slip out of political life and return to his own personal, scholarly interest and pursuits. It is told that on the return trip from Mexico to his home city, he had stopped by the way to measure the altitudes of mountains, collect plants and seeds, and visit the newly discovered ruins of Mitla. From that trip he brought back, too, a portrait of President Washington, which he presented to be hung in the hall where the Assembly met. He had written books on commerce, political economy, and law. Now he renewed correspondence with his French and British scientific friends, and doubtless considered his public life finished. In 1834, however, he was chosen by election President of the Republic. He was not to take office, for on March second he died, at the age of fifty-four. He had served brilliantly in both the colonial and separatist periods, and contributed largely toward the winning of independence and the establishment of the republican form of government.

DELGADO OF SALVADOR

DELGADO OF SALVADOR

At the time of his death the Legislative Assembly voted that he be called the "Father of His Country."

LITTLE El Salvador, smallest of the Central American Republics, a beautiful tropical country lying wholly on the Pacific, has always had a way of being first to do things. In 1937 it was the first republic to complete a section of the Pan American highway, due to stretch the entire length of both continents. In 1811 it was the first to raise the cry of independence from Spain, and the man who sounded the *grito* was a benevolent, high-born scholar, whose bust adorns the Salvador niche in the Pan American Gallery of Patriots in Washington.

HIS FAMILY AND EDUCATION

It is pleasant to meet such a man as José Matias Delgado in those times of strife. Yet the peace that shines from his calm features was of his own making, for he lived in troubled times. Born on February 24, 1767, he was of noble Spanish lineage, his father, Don Pedro Delgado, being of the family of the Lords of Polan in Toledo, and his mother, Doña Maria Ana de León, being daughter of a leading Salvadorean family claiming direct descent from the first *alcade* (local administrator) of Guatemala after the Conquest. All five of the Central American republics, Honduras, Nicaragua, Costa Rica, and El Salvador, as well as Guatemala, were still, in José Delgado's boyhood, part of the political Captaincy-General of Guatemala, which included eight provinces of what is now Mexico.

There was a pleasant social life in San Salvador, its chief town, two thousand feet above the sea coast, where he grew up. It was a Spanish-American town of the best traditions, with its gaieties, its churches, and its intellectual and political leaders. From it José took the step natural for such a boy, of going across the border to Guatemala City, where he entered the Seminary, winning a scholarship to pay for his tuition and living, and then went on to the university.

Young Delgado did well in his studies and was liked by his fellow students, as well as being approved by his teachers. He took his degree of Bachelor of Philosophy and then stayed on for courses in theology and law, doing so well in his classes that in his last year he was called on to substitute for some of his professors when they were obliged to be absent. At the end of his course of study he was a Doctor of Laws, but he chose to enter the service of the Church rather than the courts. After his ordination as a priest, he returned to his birthplace, San Salvador, to minister to a parish there.

JOSÉ MATIAS DELGADO
1767 - 1832
From the bust in the Gallery of Patriots, Washington, D. C.

PASTOR AND PATRIOT

The young pastor became dearly beloved by his people. He spent his own personal fortune for the poor and needy, and came by his spiritual power to be adviser and counselor for people of all ranks of life. There was no man in the town who was more respected than the young scholar-priest.

His influence was, therefore, great when he spoke on political matters. These were times of decision for all the colonies of Spain. In spite of the efforts of the few Spanish officials to suppress the news, word came through of the uprisings in South America and Mexico which were following the news of a French Bonaparte on the throne. The royalists in Central America were ready to follow the lead of the Spaniards of the mother country who were declaring their own Ferdinand VII to be lawful sovereign and setting up a Regency to govern for him until Spain was free again.

But there were Independents, of whom Father Delgado was one, who felt that now was the long-looked-for time to claim the right of self-government for the colonies. Nor did these patriots lack grievances. A new Captain-General arrived from Montevideo who had seen the insurrections in the Argentine region and was determined to check any such tendencies in Central America. From the time of his coming, in the spring of 1811, all intelligent native-born leaders were under suspicion. Spies were set to watch and listen in every company and at every gathering. On the slightest suspicion citizens were thrown into prison or exiled. The hopes which had been raised of a new, free age, under the people's *junta* in Spain, were disappointed. Here was a worse despotism than had been endured in the past, and it was being practised at a time when the North American colonies had been free for a generation, and all South America and Mexico were aflame with revolution.

THE FIRST CENTRAL AMERICAN REVOLT

The moment came when reinforcements of money and muskets arrived in San Salvador for the Spanish troops quartered there. Six men had agreed on the plan of action, with Delgado as the leading spirit. On November 5, 1811, they roused their following and seized the 3,000 new muskets and the $200,000.00 just arrived from the royal treasury. One of their number, Don Manuel José Arcé, proclaimed national independence, and invitations were sent to other towns of the province to join in the movement.

Several towns responded eagerly, while others refused. It has been said that the revolt would have spread all through El Salvador and into Guatemala if it had not been for a wise Spanish secretary of government. He made terms with the town council, dismissed several local Spanish officials whose high-handed acts had angered the people, and agreed on a political amnesty for the leaders. It must have been plain to them that the people were not yet ready for the final act. Yet they had voiced the call, which was never, from that time on, completely silenced.

Delgado was transferred to Guatemala City, where he could be kept under careful watch by the authorities. In the years which he spent there, he managed, however, to keep up a constant activity for future freedom. He was there to help in guiding the wider movement when, in 1821, the real separation came.

We are so familiar with the civil wars and the bloodshed which followed the winning of independence in Central America that it is always a surprise to recall with what absence of violence the actual change came. Perhaps these wise, moderate patriot leaders were partly responsible for the easy transition. Certainly, too, the time was ripe. The Spanish Government came to know that it could not hold this "middle land" between the two continents with South America and Mexico both on the point of freedom.

THE DEMAND FOR FREEDOM

The Liberal Constitution which was forced on King Ferdinand VII in 1820 granted to both Spain and the colonies a considerable measure of freedom and self-government. The leaders of Central America were ready for it. In 1818 the tyrannical Captain-General who had roused so much opposition was removed. In 1820 a Spanish Brigadier-General, Gavino Gainza, came to Guatemala bringing the royal proclamation, and by July a provincial council was meeting in the capital. With Delgado the acknowledged leader of one party, and another able leader, José del Valle, a Honduran, at the head of another political group, there was opportunity for public debate on the problems of Central America and the need of reforms.

The leaders did not move rashly. They sent across the water to the meeting of the Spanish *Cortes* in June, 1821, their American representatives, who offered to that body the terms of a future peace. It was made plain that the colonials were determined to be treated as free men, with constitutional rights of self-government. They insisted, too, that the rules of trade should be changed, to give Americans equal rights with the Spaniards in Europe in such commerce, and that native-born Americans should be as eligible for public offices as were the Spaniards. If these rights were granted, the Central Americans offered, in return, to make large annual payments on Spain's national debt, and to help in the support of the royal navy.

No colonials ever made more fair offers to a mother country. If the Spanish government had been stronger, or there had been no other revolution going on at the time, some agreement might have been reached. But the tide for freedom had begun to sweep in. No man or group of men could have stopped it. By September the people themselves were roused, as they had not been in the days when Delgado and the others began to plan.

THE DECLARATION

In the events of that September of 1821, each one of the famous band of Central American patriots played his own important part. Delgado seems always to have been the one to persuade others to action, and to act as peace-maker. At the last there was haste, for up in Mexico Iturbide had seized the leadership, and he was inviting adjoining provinces to come into his new, grand State. Already some of the border provinces had agreed. The Guatemalans saw that they must act at once.

They went about it cleverly. The elderly Spanish Cap-tain-General was persuaded to give up his authority to General Gainza. Then Delgado was set to convince Gainza that he would best serve his country and his own ends as well by coöperating with the plans. He was a man who liked to hold offices, and he was promised the presidency of the new government if he would accept the separation from Spain as inevitable and lead off in the new State.

When the time came, the people themselves settled the matter. On September fourteenth Gainza summoned the high officials of the government to meet on the following day and decide what should be done in response to the growing excitement among the people. All that night the word was spread abroad, and by eight o'clock the next morning the courtyard and porticos and antechambers of the government house were filled with a growing throng, through whom the arriving officials had to pass. There were two parties among the Independents, one, led by Delgado, favoring immediate action; the other counseling delay till the rest of the country was consulted. When the voting began, each vote for immediate independence was greeted by the crowd with applause; each vote for delay, with groans. The anti-Independents withdrew from the assembly, fearing for their lives if they protested before the excited people.

When the voting was over, the Declaration of Independence had been approved by all the members present. It stated the desire of Guatemala—that is, of the entire Spanish Captaincy-General—to become a free and independent nation, and invited all citizens to choose representatives for a national congress.

AS HEAD OF EL SALVADOR

Delgado had signed the Declaration. He was next sent back by the new government to calm a disturbance in his native San Salvador. The patriots there had followed the Guatemala City announcement, as soon as they heard of it, by declaring El Salvador a free and absolutely independent state. But though the Spanish official in charge there had seemed at first to yield, he had retaliated the next day by throwing the Independent leaders, among them Manuel Arcé, into prison. Delgado began as soon as he entered the province to liberate prisoners in the towns through which he passed. The people followed him as he came toward the capital, and the Spanish official who had refused to recognize the Declaration was sent away. With Delgado's assuming the headship of the province, peace followed. He was back once more in his homeland and in his own city.

This was the opportunity for which Delgado had longed. He and his provincial council began at once to work for the good of the little country, starting a system of primary schools and putting the government finances in order. But this tranquillity was not to last. Iturbide of Mexico was determined to annex Central America. The Guatemalan *junta,* meeting under Gainza, decided that this was the best course for the new Central American state, and proceeded to accept for the whole country. But Salvador never let anyone act for it. Delgado's committee protested to the Guatemalans, and when their protest was not heeded, proceeded to take up arms and resist the army, under General Filisola, which came down from Mexico to bring the region into the empire.

This opposition was doubtless one of the causes of the downfall of Iturbide's dreams. But in the year and more before his empire came to an end, Salvador, though defeated by General Filisola's larger armies, made one more attempt to avoid annexation with Mexico. In a petition signed by thousands of Indians and Spanish Americans, it expressed its desire to be annexed to the United States, and appealed for protection and help. The United States was the head, it said, of the "great republican family," and might therefore keep it from the fate which it was resisting of becoming a part of the Mexican empire. The government at Washington was too much concerned over its own affairs, having recently acquired vast lands in the Louisiana Purchase, to pay much attention to this honor paid it by the stanch, republican little state. Fortunately, the empire of Iturbide fell, and within fifteen months of the Guatemalan acceptance of the Mexican proposition, the relation between the countries was dissolved by mutual consent.

THE NATIONAL CONGRESS OF 1823

It is pleasant to remember that General Filisola, who had been sent south to carry through the annexation by arms, if need be, now called on all Central Americans to send delegates to a national Congress to decide their national future. The delegates came together on June 24, 1823, with Delgado in the chair as President. The following week they declared the provinces to be free, independent states, with no allegiance to Spain, Mexico, or any other power, and planned to form a Central American Federation. This act of July first President Delgado was the first to sign. The union was not to succeed, but it was a brave effort.

Father Delgado's last years were spent in El Salvador. The new Central American Federation, which started off so bravely, was split almost immediately with dissension. The two parties, which under different names were to continue their strife for many years, began to shape themselves as Conservatives and Liberals. They could unite on such measures as spreading education among the Indian and *mestizo* populations. But the Church, long dominated from Spain, was the stronghold of tradition. Delgado persuaded the Liberals in El Salvador, who were always ready to act independently of Guatemala, to make their province a separate diocese, of which he was appointed the first bishop. This made trouble with the Archbishop at Guatemala City, and there began the political dissensions which were shortly to lead to civil war. No man could share in the political life of those troubled times without losing old friends and making bitter enemies, and Delgado was not the man to compromise when independence was at stake.

"FATHER OF HIS COUNTRY"

When, however, the eminent Salvadorean died on November 12, 1832, after an illness which he had recognized for some time as fatal, the people of both city and State mourned as for a father. He had grown up among them. He had come to them as a young pastor and priest, and been their friend in all their times of need. The Legislative Assembly was voicing the thoughts of the people when it voted that henceforth he should be called the "Father of His Country." In his last days he had called to him a group of the leading men of the city and made them swear that they would go to all lengths, even to death itself, rather than let their country lose its liberty. In the coming years they were often to recall Delgado and that promise.

FATHER SIMEON CANAS

FATHER SIMEON CANAS

"The entire nation has been declared free; so should be the individuals who compose it."—Canas.

THERE are some facts which it is well for North Americans to remember. One is that Central America led all the civilized nations of the world in abolishing slavery. Another is that Bolívar and his associates hesitated about inviting the United States to join in the first Pan American Congress because it was a slave-holding nation, and so powerful that its delegates might retard the progress of individual human freedom which the progressive leaders of the new southern republics were trying to write into their constitutions.

There are also days in Pan American history which belong to all Americans. One of these is the day in 1823, December fourteenth, when Dr. José Simeon Canas, one of the nation's most distinguished and beloved leaders, came before the newly formed National Assembly of Central America, and in a moving speech proposed the writing into the constitution of the prohibition against slavery.

A MAN OF FAMILY AND DISTINCTION

Canas was of all men the one to make this proposal, for he had long stood for progressive and liberal ideas. His family were among the wealthiest in the province of El Salvador. His father, Don Pablo de Canas, and his mother, Doña Lucia de Villacorta, owned a large and valuable estate, on which they lived much of the year, going to Guatemala City for the rainy season. For the sake of educating their four boys, of whom José Simeon was the third, they stayed longer and longer each year in the city, and Simeon went through the famous Colegio de San Francisco de Borja, took advanced degrees, and then went on into teaching. In 1803 he was chosen to be President of the University of Guatemala, over which he was presiding when many of the younger patriot leaders came there for their education. A man of broad sympathies, he tried to improve education in the colony and to spread learning under the Spanish rule. With other colonials he rejoiced in the brief period of liberal government after the Constitution of 1812 was adopted in Spain, and was vastly disturbed when Ferdinand VII restored the old restrictions on personal liberty.

Because Canas was a man of weight in the community, his words were always heard with respect in the councils of the government. It was on his motion and by his personal persuasion that the elderly and ineffective Captain-General from Spain was led to hand over his authority to General Gainza, who was finally prevailed upon to call the celebrated council which on September 15, 1821, adopted the Declaration of Independence, and he was a member of the National Constituent Assembly which met in June of 1823, with José Matias Delgado as president, set up the Central American Federation, and remained in session for nineteen months, framing a constitution for the new government.

NEGROES IN CENTRAL AMERICA

It was in this body, with its sixty-four deputies, that Dr. Canas made his famous and moving plea for the abolition of slavery. There were at the time only about a thousand negroes in the entire colony, as the work on the *haciendas* was performed mostly by Indians, whose lot was far from easy. But no effort was made at this time to improve their conditions of labor. They had not been denied the vote, but by the Spanish code of 1810 the descendants of Africans had been refused the rights of citizenship. There had been protest in the national *Cortes* in Spain when they had been so excluded. Some of the deputies from the South American colonies had sought their freedom, declaring that many of these men had done valuable service as priests, and in other callings, and had fought bravely in the armies. But at that time one of the deputies for Guatemala had protested that the black men were not ready for full citizenship. The final vote had been, at that time, that only men whose private and public lives had proved them worthy should have the vote.

HIS PLEA FOR THE ABOLITION OF SLAVERY

It was against this background of opinion that Father Canas came before the Assembly with his plea. He had been ill, and came with great effort, as he indicated in his opening words. "I come," he said, "with feeble steps, but even if I were at death's door, from death's door would I come to propose to you a measure on behalf of helpless human beings. . . . I beseech you, before you do anything else, to proclaim in today's session the emancipation of our brothers in slavery."

He proceeded to discuss the setting up of a fund to pay the owners of slaves, in case they had purchased the men and women now considered their property, and then went on with his plea.

"We all know that our brothers have been violently deprived of the inestimable gift of liberty, that they groan in servitude, sighing for a kindly hand to break the bonds of slavery. Nothing, then, will give greater glory to this august assembly, more satisfaction to the nation, or more benefit to our brothers, than the prompt proclamation of their liberty, which is manifestly just and should be decreed without discussion and by general acclaim. The entire nation has been declared free; so should be the individuals who compose it."

Father Canas had been reduced from his boyhood condition of wealth in his long years of public service. At this time he was in particularly difficult circumstances financially because of inability to collect from the treasury of the new government moneys due him for months and years. Yet he announced that he would gladly yield whatever was owed to him in order to start the fund for the indemnity of owners of slaves.

When he sat down after this long speech, the entire house applauded enthusiastically, and the vote to incorporate such action in the new constitution was unanimously adopted. Laws passed within the next few months not only emancipated all slaves but declared free any slaves coming to Central America from other countries. This last provision was important considering the nearness of Caribbean islands where large numbers of negroes worked on the great plantations.

This was one of the last appearances of Simeon Canas in the Assembly. He suffered an attack of paralysis which confined him to his home, but the men active in politics came to him there for counsel. He was a relative and close friend of Delgado, and stood by him in his later difficulties, publishing many articles on current happenings. Early in his life he had taken Church orders. Now in his home he carried on his priestly office, giving time and counsel to those in need, and dispensing a wide charity. There was need of such service in those troubled years of civil war and distress. Father Canas died on March 4, 1838, fifteen years after his most famous speech, but by that speech he is best remembered, as he would doubtless have chosen to be.

LARREINAGA OF NICARAGUA

LARREINAGA OF NICARAGUA

"The soul of the gatherings of insurgents that call themselves patriots and cherish the idea of independence in these countries."—Bustamente.

THE nearness of Central America and Mexico to Europe, even in the days of slow sailing vessels, is always a surprise. To find the bust of a Central American statesman who died a century ago in one of the galleries of the Sorbonne, the University of Paris, is to be reminded of the fact that the world of scholars was in those days a united world. It was one of the complaints of the Church that the revolutionary ideas of the men of letters of France could not be kept out of New Spain in spite of the ocean that separated the colonies from the continent of Europe. The poets and artists of Mexico were known and honored in Paris; and this Central American scholar, Miguel Larreinaga, who studied the volcanoes which formed the backbone of the Isthmus and wrote a book on "The Fire of the Volcanoes," was admired by the German naturalist-traveler, Alexander von Humboldt, and had his work translated into several languages.

There has never been a more patriotic group of men than the company which sat down in the council chamber of Guatemala and planned a new government which should succeed the Spanish colonial rule, and few countries could have produced as many university men who were ready to drop all their affairs and attend for long periods of time and at personal sacrifice to the country's business.

BEFORE THE DAYS OF INDEPENDENCE

Miguel Larreinaga was fifty years old at the time when independence came to Central America. Born on the twenty-ninth of September, 1771, he was brought up by his grandparents on his mother's side of the family, for his mother died at his birth and his father had died a few months earlier.

He went to school in León, the farthest north of the three Nicaraguan cities on the Pacific slopes. All Central America faced west in those days, and Nicaragua most of all, for though it stretched from ocean to ocean, its eastern coast was low and swampy for from twenty to fifty miles inland from the coast, with dense virgin forest farther in the interior. The British had lumbering camps here and laid claim to the unpopulated regions where only the Mosquito Indians had homes and occasional villages. But on the Pacific side the coast was bold and rocky, with two excellent harbors, and back from the water there was the strip of fertile country where the population centered. The rivalry between the cities of León and Granada which was to tear the country to

MIGUEL LARREINAGA
1771 - 1847

pieces in the days of the republics had not risen to such a pitch in the days of Miguel's childhood.

At the University of San Carlos in Guatemala City, from which Miguel graduated with honors in 1798, he showed his brilliant mind and the passion for learning which was to keep him always a student until the end of his long life. With it went a love of sharing his knowledge, which turned him to teaching. Like other patriots he felt the need for education in Central America, but while they worked at arms' length by training teachers or passing laws, Larreinaga spent years in teaching in the government schools of both Nicaragua and Guatemala, and became a great favorite with the young men in his classes.

As time went on, however, he turned more and more to the practice of law and to parliamentary debate, and in this field he incurred the enmity of the Spanish authorities. A particularly obnoxious and tyrannical administrator had come out from Spain, one José de Bustamente, who set up a system of spying on all suspected of independent views. It was this man who expressed his annoyance at Larreinaga's actions in the words quoted at the opening of the chapter. The patriots were meeting both openly and secretly, and the lawyer-teacher was undoubtedly the "soul of the gatherings." It was said that Bustamente kept him from the office of Judge of the Royal Academy to which he had been given an appointment in 1814.

A VISIT TO EUROPE

When deputies were chosen in that same year to go to Spain to represent Central America, the well-known young lawyer was elected to represent not only his own Nicaragua, but also El Salvador and Quezaltenango. The people felt he could be trusted with their interests in Madrid.

Larreinaga stayed in Europe for three years. Before he left he gave to the University of León his unusually complete library, containing more than three thousand books. The wonder is not so much in the gift, which was in accord with his generous spirit, but in a library of so many volumes collected in Central America at a time when books were so scarce.

As a scholar he was completely happy in Europe, getting intense satisfaction from his relations with universities and with other men of learning and culture. But at Madrid he was much disturbed by the treatment of the American deputies. For himself he did not mind, but for his country and his colleagues he was indignant at the lack of attention paid to the just claims of the colonies. The work which patriot meetings with his friends had begun in Central America was completed here. He returned to Guatemala in August of 1821 convinced that his country must become independent, and that from this moment he must devote his time and effort unstintedly toward that end.

AT THE SEPTEMBER MEETING

Again and again we come back in our story to that September Fifteenth when the Declaration of Independence was made. Larreinaga was in the company called by the Spanish Governor, Brigadier-General Gabino Gainza, to the reception hall of the Palace at eight o'clock in the morning of that great day. There he met friends whom he had not seen since his return.

The question which was debated was that of immediate action or delay until the other provinces should be consulted. It was a reasonable question, but as the debate went on those seeking independence saw that delay would be only an excuse for failing to act. One of the strongest opponents of action was a churchman, Archbishop Casaus, who declared that it was "absurd, criminal, and sinful" to break away from Spain. The argument grew heated. If discussion continued in this spirit, the vote would finally be taken in such bitterness that no good would result.

Then Larreinaga, only recently returned from Spain, appeared on the platform, calm, strong, kindly, but with arguments which cut through all the talk like a keen sword thrust. The noisy audience quieted while he set forth the reasons why immediate action was wise and complete separation necessary. This man had been in Spain as their country's representative. Report had it that he had been held in high honor there for his learning and legal skill. Yet he was advocating separation from the mother country. When he had finished his speech, the vote was taken, and independence was declared. His words had helped greatly in bringing the assembly to harmony.

AS LAWYER AND JURIST

All these accomplishments might have been credited to Larreinaga, and the tale have been complete. But this was only the year 1821, and he was to serve his country for another twenty-five and more years. He was sent to the Mexican Congress called by Iturbide during the brief time when the Central American provinces were joining in that empire. When that empire was abruptly dissolved and republican institutions were again to be established, the Mexicans did not want to spare this wise and distinguished jurist and lawmaker. He stayed on for a dozen years, holding important offices in the State of Oaxaca, home of Benito Juarez, serving in the *Audiencia* of the State, and as district judge, and also as assessor general of Chiapas and magistrate in its Court of Justice. The record of his labors was a new testimony to his high-minded devotion to the cause of good government and his extraordinary capacity. In these years he collected another library which he presented, on his departure for Guatemala in 1835, to the State of Oaxaca. In gratitude for his services as jurist and teacher, one of his students wrote a long poem, in the verse form of a Latin eclogue, which narrates his contributions to the State and to his pupils and recites in glowing terms the admiration of all for their *"maestro, el Licenciado Don Miguel Larreinaga."* From the yellowed pages of that testimonial, reprinted at the time of his death, we may read of the honor in which this Central American was held in Mexico.

The list of public offices which he held in the years following his return to his native land shows how eagerly he was welcomed there. The new republics had many questions to settle concerning commerce and local trade, and his decisions in the courts were the basis for new laws. He is remembered as a great parliamentary orator, known for the graciousness of his manner and the clearness of his language. As time went on he filled judgeships, and his pronouncements were noted for their vast learning in the laws of the past and their exact interpretation for the present. Guatemala entrusted to him the task of revising its Civil Code, which was burdened with much that was reactionary and unjust. He worked on this for years, and the adoption of his report was voted on the seventeenth anniversary of independence, September 15, 1838.

This was the year when the Indian Carrera had brought his horde of followers into Guatemala City, and on the occasion of the celebration and the adoption of the new code, Larreinaga gave a famous discourse in which he denounced in no uncertain terms the conduct of

Carrera as being outside the law and therefore causing the ruin of Central America.

So the list of his deeds and services goes on, with him as Foreign Minister for Guatemala, and finally Regent of the Supreme Court. In all these offices he held strongly to his Liberal views, opposing always the Aristocratic party which refused to trust the people with the government. At the time of his death on April 28, 1847, this Nicaraguan was greatly honored by his fellow citizens, and as the years went on, he became, as the Central American historian puts it, "one of the most venerated figures in the history of the country." A century later he has been chosen the representative citizen for Nicaragua in the Gallery of Patriots at Washington.

MORAZÁN, CHAMPION OF FEDERATION

MORAZÁN, CHAMPION OF FEDERATION

"Morazán will stand in history as in many respects the best, and in all the ablest, man that Central America had."—Hubert Howe Bancroft, historian.

TO North Americans of a hundred years ago the name "Central America" stood for "revolutions"—not for revolution against Spain, since that had been carried through earlier and with little bloodshed, but for revolutions which took place in provinces and republics of which they barely knew the names. There was some commerce to this neck of land between the continents. The government at Washington was interested in getting control of a canal route across Nicaragua or Panama. The newspapers carried reports of remarkable ruins of ancient cities recently discovered in the jungles. But the most frequent news was of changes of rulers in the newly created federation of states, and there were disturbing tales of violent civil war. Even in Washington no one was clear how best to proceed in dealing with these neighbors to the south whose independence from Spain the United States had recognized so gladly in the 1820's.

AN AMERICAN OBSERVER

Fortunately for our present knowledge of the Central Americans of this period, several men of ability traveled through those parts on errands of one sort or another. One of them, John L. Stephens, was a trained observer and ready writer, and it is to him that we owe a vivid personal portrait of the man whom he considered the "best man in Central America," Francisco Morazán, who belongs to all the Central American republics because of his efforts to unite them, but especially to Honduras, where he was born. Mr. Stephens was an official observer, for President Van Buren made him United States Minister just as he was preparing to sail on a trip for investigation of the newly discovered ancient ruins. He was a native of New Jersey and graduate of Columbia College in New York, who had spent five years in travel in European and Mediterranean countries and written popular books describing his adventures. When the man who had just been appointed to the diplomatic post died suddenly in 1839, the President did well to give the appointment to Mr. Stephens, desiring him to make personal observations of the conditions in these lands and report back to him what he found there. He was instructed to present his official credentials to the government or governments he found. He made his tour, found his jungle-covered ruins, was tremendously interested in the country and its people, but never in the course of a journey of eight or nine months found any government sufficiently secure or established for him to decide to recognize it in the name of the United States. In those countries of violent party warfare there was too much danger of tying himself up with the wrong party and becoming the victim of its defeat for him to make the decision safely.

The man to whom he would have liked to present his credentials was Francisco Morazán, who had been president of the loosely united republics for eight years. But General Morazán was almost at the end of his career when Mr. Stephens had the good fortune to meet him, and his enemies were hard on his trail.

A NATIVE OF HONDURAS

Morazán was a Honduran, born on October 3, 1792 in Tegucigalpa, the oldest city of Central America and the present capital of the republic. Its history in the early days centered around the wealth in the nearby mountains. Here were the rich silver mines which attracted to the region conquistadores, Spanish governors and their followers, and pirates and adventurers all down the centuries following the landing of Columbus on the Honduran coast. Francisco's father was of French ancestry, a French Creole from one of the West Indies. His mother was a native of Tegucigalpa.

To his father's side of the family he owed his florid complexion and light blue eyes, and perhaps, also, his intellectual activity. The historian Bancroft, who came in the later nineteenth century to have intimate knowledge of this region and its leaders through his Spanish researches, tells of his youth and young manhood.

His education was such as he could obtain in the country at the time; but his quickness of apprehension and thirst for knowledge soon placed him far above his countrymen. He was of impetuous temperament, and possessed at the same time great decision and perseverance. His bearing was free and manly, and his manner frank and open. These qualities could not fail to and did secure him the love and respect of his fellow-citizens, giving him an immense influence over them.

Morazán did not stay in Tegucigalpa, but went as a youth to the beautiful Spanish city of Comayagua, which had been founded in 1540 on a plain in the highlands. Here in his time there was much wealth, with a university, a cathedral, and the fine houses which belonged to a capital of the old-time Spanish empire. He became a shopman, and then a clerk in a notary's office. When independence came in 1821, he was ready for holding office under the new government.

THE HONDURAS DECREE

Honduras declared its independence of Spain in September of 1821, when the papers from Guatemala City reached the city of Comayagua. In order to catch the spirit of the times, and share in Morazán's devotion to his cause, it is well to read the declaration as it was given to the people.

FRANCISCO MORAZÁN
1792 - 1842
From the bust in the Gallery of Patriots, Washington, D. C.

Your Governor, Provincial Assembly, and City Council, jointly with you, swore independence from Spanish rule on the 28th of this month, the first day of our political regeneration, from which our future happiness will flow.

This era will bring forth the most precious of fruits: the perfect union and brotherhood of our provinces, confuting the mistaken opinions of our opponents; true justice, bringing us into close touch with the supreme government which will uphold this principle; the stimulation of all branches of agriculture, mining, manufacturing and commerce; and, finally, liberty to enjoy the land where it has pleased the Omnipotent to set us, the richest and most fertile soil of the world, which leaves nothing to be desired.

This auspicious day, this happy moment should be devoted, first of all, to giving thanks to the Sovereign Author of all good at a mass which it has been agreed to celebrate solemnly tomorrow in the cathedral and which members of all official organizations should attend; and tonight and the two following nights there will be illuminations and public diversions.

Union, Comayagua, peace, and may no other sound be heard than the cry: Bravo for Independence! This means peace and union, and he who thinks otherwise will be held a traitor to the State.

Comayagua, September 30, 1821.

Such was the enthusiasm with which the Honduran leaders adopted the resolution proposed at Guatemala City. It is to be noticed that they declared themselves independent of Spain, but accepted no other tie, save that of "union." There was no unity to be taken for granted in the several parts of the Spanish Captaincy-General which stretched from Mexico to Panama and the Pacific Ocean to the Caribbean Sea. Such union as was to come was to be the result of strenuous efforts on the part of the republic's leaders, and of them all none was more active than Francisco Morazán. He was prominent then in Honduras, as is shown by his holding in 1824, when he was only thirty-two years old, the position of Secretary-General, and he was later Senator from the republic, and at one time its acting head.

THE TWO PARTIES

In the story of these years, and of the men in each of the present republics who were leaders during the federation of them all into a Central American republic, it is necessary to remember that the political life was divided not by countries chiefly, though there were strong local loyalties, but by two parties, bitterly opposed to each other and each one determined to rule. They appear under different names, but the difference is always the same. There were the Centralists (or the Aristocrats, or Serviles) led by members of colonial families and by priests and churchmen, who clung to the old ways and sought to replace Spanish rule by a local government carrying on the same autocratic practises. Their power came from the influence of the priests over the Indians, who made up a large part of the population of some of the provinces. These dark-skinned natives had carried their superstitious beliefs and fanatic devotion to religion into their obedient service of the Church. They cared nothing for the political debates which went on in the halls of state, nor did they understand the meaning of elections and the ballot. But they could be roused to the highest reaches of excitement by any fancied attack on their religion or its leaders.

> From the time of the conquest [says Stephens] Guatemala had remained in a state of profound tranquillity as a colony of Spain. The Indians submitted quietly to the authority of the whites, and all bowed to the divine right of the Romish church. . . . The Central party consisted of a few leading families, which by reason of certain privileges of monopoly for importations under the old Spanish government, assumed the tone of nobles, sustained by the priests and friars, and the religious feeling of the country. . . . The Centralists wished to preserve the usages of the colonial system, and resisted every innovation and every attack, direct or indirect, upon the privileges of the Church, and their own prejudices or interests.

The Liberals, on the other hand, were the broader, more progressive, more enlightened citizens, who were active in introducing reforms and setting up a republic after the pattern of the United States and other free governments. Their opposition to the local Church is not to be wondered at, for it was against free, democratic government and held vast properties away from both people and State, but they were always for its reform, not for its downfall. If the struggle had been only between whites, such a distinction would have been within the range of possible understanding. Among the Indian population there proved to be no such possibility. To them any effort to limit the power of the Church in political life was an attack on religion.

AS HEAD OF THE FEDERATION

Morazán was a Liberal, destined to be soon the leader of the Liberal party in its military as well as political activities. As such he came in 1828 and 1829 into armed conflict with the federal forces who were maintaining Centralist rule in Guatemala City, which was the capital at that time for Central America. In 1828 he assisted the Salvadorean Liberals in gaining control of their local government, and then marched with an army of Liberals of Salvador and Honduras against the capital. A first defeat was soon followed by victory, and in February of 1829, after only three days of siege, he took possession of the city.

He proceeded to set up a Liberal government for the entire republic with a harsh treatment of his political opponents which was to become characteristic of all Central American dictatorships. All leaders of the Central party were banished or fled in advance of such enforced exile; the convents were abolished; the orders of friars were disbanded and the friars were put on board vessels and shipped out of the country; and the archbishop fled. Defending himself at a later date, Morazán said: "No one was put to death, or had money exacted from him by me. . . . Duty gave way to magnanimity, and there was no cause to regret it."

The "duty" had taken on strange forms, according to our modern standards. "There was but one side to politics in Guatemala," wrote Mr. Stephens a decade later. "Both parties had a beautiful way of producing unanimity of opinion by driving out of the country all who did not agree with them." Morazán's method was particularly high-handed. He once invited the leaders of the Centralists to a reception at his official residence. They came to the audience chamber in elegant attire, expecting a conference with the new President on affairs of state. Instead, a company of soldiers came into the room where they were assembled and arrested them, taking them to a Pacific port, where they were put forcibly aboard a vessel about to embark for Panama. It was a convenient method of ridding oneself of political enemies, and Morazán could properly point to the fact that he did not have them all shot, as his successor, the Indian dictator Carrera, would have done. Indeed, the unfortunate boatload lived to harass him later, as did other political exiles. These men compelled the ship's captain to change his course and take them to Mexico, from which place they planned and plotted to return and seize control of the government.

It is to be remembered, too, that while the friars were

sent away, there were exceptions where no political action was suspected. Those of the Order of Mercy were allowed to remain, as were also of the Bethlehemite Hospitallers, who devoted their time to teaching and to the care of convalescents.

General Morazán had no intention of keeping the country under military law longer than was necessary for the establishing of the new Liberal government. It is even said that he entered Guatemala City, after its capture, with the flag in one hand and the Constitution in the other. He called together the Federal Congress, which met late in March of the year following his entrance into Guatemala City. He also installed at that time a Supreme Court, and prepared for an election. In that election he and Valle received by far the largest number of votes, making him President and Valle Vice-President. That autumn of 1830, on the eve of the ninth anniversary of national independence, Morazán made a triumphal entry into Guatemala City, where the outgoing President turned over the office to him. There were no signs of personal triumph, save such as the people gave. He was inaugurated with republican simplicity amid scenes of celebration of the national holiday, and all the States of the Federation sent their congratulations to President Morazán.

HIS PROGRAM OF REFORM

If only there had been a chance for these Liberals to carry through their programs of reform! That is what one feels as one watches the tragedy of the 1830's follow the high hopes of the early 1820's. Morazán did so many good things. He endeavored to improve education, setting up public schools all over the country on the Lancastrian system, which was then being adopted in the United States and several South American countries. By this method, brought from the mill towns of England, pupil teachers could assist the single trained teacher, and so help in the handling of large numbers of children without too great expense. He introduced new law codes, copied from the latest practise in the United States, to replace the ancient Spanish procedures, and tried to establish trial by jury.

These reforms would have worked well if the people had been ready for them. But even the Creoles had had little or no chance to gain experience in self-government during the three hundred years of Spanish rule. Nor was it a country which Nature had united. The mountain and jungle barriers seemed set to oppose union of the uplands and the lowlands, the east coast and the west, the Pacific shores and those of the Atlantic. A country united only by mule paths had little chance to form a strong and successful federation of provinces.

Moreover, the party bitterness was intense, and the harsh measures of putting down defeated opponents served only to increase it. The countries which were to become independent republics seceded from the Union at will, and then were pulled back into it by force or persuasion. Morazán won his second term as President, but in those years the Centralists were gaining strength. The leaders had slipped back into the country from Mexico and Panama. They had worked constantly with those of their party who remained. The President might, by the power of his personality, have held the separate groups together longer if it had not been for an outside event, an "Act of God," as the old law phrase has it, over which Morazán had no control.

THE EPIDEMIC—AND CARRERA

An epidemic of cholera, the first ever to visit Central America, swept the country, and the people were crazed with terror as it spread from village to village. The government sent doctors to help the stricken people and halt the spread of the illness, and the priests took advantage of the horror to turn the people against the Liberals. The doctors washed their instruments in water to cleanse them, and the priests declared that these doctors and other Liberals had poisoned the wells and caused the epidemic. Morazán had encouraged an English attempt to bring in immigrants and colonize. The cry now raised was that the government was poisoning the waters and spreading the disease in order to kill off the natives and make room for foreigners.

A leader now appeared from among the Indians, Rafael Carrera, a full-blooded Indian who had been a drummer in a Centralist regiment, but had retired to his native village after the Liberal victories, to keep pigs. This man, who was to be the ruler of Guatemala for many years, came first into view as the leader of an outbreak immediately after the epidemic in which the Indians rose against the Liberals.

That was the beginning of the movement which was to drive Morazán and his party from power. With the war cry, *"Viva la religión y muerte a los estranjeros!"* (Long live religion and death to the foreigners!), this ignorant Indian, with great natural ability as a leader, went up and down the countryside, collecting discontented men in his bands of marauders. Without the help of the priests and Centralists he could have done little more than carry on an outlaw reign of terror. But there was dissension in the Liberal party. President Morazán had been forced to move the seat of the Federal government to San Salvador. The crisis came when Carrera, at the head of a great horde of Indians, with whom other insurgents had joined, marched on the city of Guatemala and entered it.

IN GUATEMALA CITY

Mr. Stephens tells of that entry as an eye-witness reported it to him. This gentleman said that he had never felt such consternation and horror as when he saw the arrival of this immense mass of barbarians, led by Carrera who was on horseback with a green bush in his hat and with his shoulders and body hung with pieces of dirty cotton cloth covered with pictures of the saints. The horde of Indians, all with green bushes in their hats, seemed at a distance like a moving forest as they choked the streets. They were armed with rusty muskets, old pistols, fowling-pieces, sticks shaped like guns, clubs, machetes, and knives tied to the ends of long poles. To add to the strange picture, there were two or three thousand women, with sacks to be used for carrying away the plunder they might find.

This army stayed only a short time and then departed at Carrera's orders when the city officials persuaded him to be satisfied with a colonel's commission, a thousand rifles, eleven thousand dollars, and an appointment as commandant of a province. From that time, however, the conflict was on. General Morazán, who was in the last year of his second term of office as President of the Federation, returned from Salvador with a Federal army of fifteen hundred men, but in spite of the terror which they had so recently experienced, the city officials were too jealous of their own powers to welcome him cordially. The spirit of the man is shown in his forbearance. He encamped outside the city until he was finally authorized by the Guatemalans to defend them. Then he marched on Carrera's forces and drove them back into the mountains. His friends and supporters urged him to come into the city and end party strife by making himself dictator, but Morazán declared that he would accept power legally or not at all. When Carrera was subdued and had signed a treaty of submission, Morazán felt

SIGNS OF THE PAST

The findings of ruins of ancient civilizations began in the early days of independence to attract hardy travelers to southern Mexico and Central America.

obliged to return to Salvador, lest by his presence he give excuse for the party cry of the opposition that he was trying to retain control for himself by the use of Federal troops. The Union was indeed doomed when its leader could not come to its support.

A MEETING WITH EACH CHIEF

In this year of 1839, Mr. Stephens, coming to Central America, happened to meet both Carrera and Morazán. He was greatly interested in the Indian chief, who at the time of his visit had regained control of Guatemala City by driving Morazán and his troops out, and was recognized as leader of the Centralist party. The young man had proved his natural ability by learning much in his two years of command. He received the American diplomat cordially, and this future ruler, who was to be absolute master of Guatemala for many years, is described as "boyish in his manners and manner of speaking, but very grave." He was about five feet, six inches in height, with straight black hair, an Indian complexion and expression, a young man only twenty-three years old in whom the American saw great promise.

It was a few weeks later, while he was up in the mountains, in a village on the edge of the province of Guatemala, that Mr. Stephens was caught in the midst of civil war and felt himself in real danger, until General Morazán and his men entered the town. "From that moment," he says, "I felt perfectly secure; then for the first time I saw something like discipline." His description of his meeting the General should be given in full.

General Morazán, with several officers, was standing in the corner of the cabildo; a large fire was burning before the door, and a table stood against the wall, with a candle and chocolate cups upon it. He was about forty-five years old, five feet ten inches high, thin, with a black moustache and week's beard, and wore a military frock-coat, buttoned up to the throat, and sword. His hat was off, and the expression of his face was mild and intelligent. Though still young, for ten years he had been the first man in the country, and for eight, President of the Republic. He had risen and had sustained himself by military skill and personal bravery; always led his forces himself; had been in innumerable battles, and often wounded, but never beaten.

The following morning General Morazán called on Mr. Stephens while he was taking his morning chocolate.

I bade him farewell [he says] with an interest greater than I had felt for any man in the country. Little did we know then the calamities that were still in store for him; that very night most of his soldiers deserted, having been kept together only by the danger to which they were exposed while in an enemy's country.

HE GOES INTO EXILE

The story of what followed is one with which any reader of Central American history of the middle of the nineteenth century is to become too tragically familiar. Yet in the case of Morazán, the dignity and sincerity of the man shine through the misfortunes through which he passed. By the time his term of office had expired most of the separate States which made up the Federation had seceded, or were on the point of so doing. He returned to Salvador to be met coldly and insulted by both the leaders and the common people on the streets. Convinced that he could not raise a new army for his fight for union, he called a public meeting and announced that he would leave the country for the good of the State and in the hope of saving the people from anarchy.

Morazán sailed from Salvador on April 5, 1841, on the schooner *Izalco,* bound for South America. At a Costa Rican port where the vessel touched, he was refused admittance by the head of the State, although several of his companions were allowed to land and set up residence. At the port of David, in Colombia, where the vessel next stopped, he issued a stirring appeal to the Central American people to see in the acts of the Centralists the danger to their country's independence and freedom. Then he went on to Chile, where he remained for two years.

RETURNS TO COSTA RICA

There he could have remained in safety for the rest of his life. But he was too valuable to the cause of the Liberals and too ardent a patriot to be content. His native state of Honduras had been one of the first to separate itself from the Federation, declaring its independence in 1838, though it was later to return to that idea. Nicaragua had suffered in 1835 a devastating earthquake and was devoting all its energies to restoration of its normal life. But Costa Rica, farther to the south, on the bend of the Isthmus toward Panama, had been enjoying comparative peace from the time of the meeting of its first assembly and the setting up of a constitution in 1825. Its freedom from the civil wars which had afflicted its neighbors was due partly to its geographical separateness, combined with its large proportion of whites, and partly to the wisdom of its chief of state, Juan Mora, who held the presidential office from 1825 for eight years, and then served in other capacities for several more years. During those years Costa Rica had served as a refuge for the political exiles from other states. But in 1838 it fell victim to the same kind of party strife which had swept the other republics. An able ruler by the name of Carillo did much for the State but made himself dictator, giving himself life tenure of office, and rousing bitter enmity among his opponents.

These Liberal Costa Ricans proceeded to invite Morazán to return and lead their resistance to Carillo. He yielded to their urgency, sailed from Panama early in 1842 and landed at a Costa Rican port with five hundred men whom he had gathered at ports of entry where he had stopped along the way. Carillo went out against him, while Morazán issued a manifesto offering Costa Ricans a rule of peace, order, and progress. The opposition seems to have been slight, and he entered the city of San José and issued a proclamation offering complete forgiveness of all political offenders and setting up a constitutional government, which was to revise the arbitrary laws of the deposed Carillo.

It is amazing to read the story of those weeks and months when it must have seemed to Morazán as if here he was to take up his lifework once more. A constituent assembly met, consisting of thirteen members, one of whom was the distinguished ex-President, Juan Mora. Morazán was promptly chosen as "acting head of the State" until a new constitution, modeled on the Liberal document of 1825, could be framed and adopted. The assembly gave to him the title of "Liberator," which he refused to accept until the lawmakers insisted.

The success of the Liberals was so great that it roused the Centralists of not only Costa Rica but Guatemala, under its dictator Carrera, to action. So powerful a man as Morazán, who could lead such a movement, must be destroyed, else the reforms would spread all over Central America. A Costa Rican revolt was begun, led by the military forces which had been influenced by these men. With the speed with which revolution gathered to itself support in those days, an army was gathered which besieged the capital, and Morazán was caught in the barracks with only a small company of soldiers. His wife was taken as she crossed one of the city's streets, but his son was still at large.

The desire of the enemy was to get Morazán out of the country, and offers were made to him of safety if he would depart. But he felt that he could not desert his cause or his followers. The fighting went on for several days, and then he and his few men managed to get out of the city one night, under cover of darkness. They reached a neighboring town but were surrounded and captured.

HIS LAST DAYS

Those last days are full of drama. He was so beloved in the town which he had reached that his captors feared the people would rise and defend him. So they deceived him by promises that his life was in no immediate danger. Meanwhile his young son, a second Francisco, followed him and was taken. The next morning an officer came to tell him and his companions that they were to be put in irons. Two of the prisoners attempted suicide, but Morazán prevented one of them from taking his life. Chained, though he was suffering from wounds, he rode on horseback in the midst of an escort of soldiers. The day happened to be September Fifteenth, and he remarked to his captors, "How solemnly we are keeping the anniversary of independence!"

There was disagreement in the councils of the victors over what should be done with him. The wiser men urged that he be given a fair trial in accordance with the law, but the more violent urged instant death. The commander yielded to their persuasions and signed an order that he should be executed in three hours. With calmness Morazán dictated to his son his last will and testament, which became, as the words fell from his lips, a declaration of faith. He had spent, he said, his own and his wife's property in the endeavor to give Costa Rica a government of laws instead of a rule of force. This was his sole offense. With the end of life so near he urged upon the youth of Central America, for which country he declared his undying love, to imitate his example and fight, if need be to redeem their land from her present plight. His last words were a disclaimer of any bitterness toward those who were ordering the sentence of death or those who should carry it out.

Francisco Morazán was shot at sunset on September 15, 1842, and there was rejoicing among his party enemies in Guatemala and Honduras as well as in Salvador and Costa Rica at the news of his death. But in all of those countries his greatness came later to be recognized. He had given his life to unite the republics, by persuasion if possible, by force if that proved necessary. That union has been attempted more than once since without lasting success. There were too many obstacles in Morazán's time. In these later years the purposes of union have been fulfilled in many respects by mutual agreements between this little group of neighbor republics. But all join in remembering the devotion of this last President of the Federation, to the good of the whole instead of the advancement of any single part of Central America. Looking back on that period they agree that the fighter-president was at that time "the best man in Central America."

GALVEZ OF GUATEMALA

GALVEZ OF GUATEMALA

"The printing press acquired for public use is, in my opinion, the best means of spreading knowledge, not so much for the young men who are dedicating themselves to a life of study, as for the public at large."—Galvez, in 1836.

WHILE Horace Mann was appealing to the Legislature of Massachusetts in the 1830's for the establishment of a Normal School for the training of teachers, President Mariano Galvez of Guatemala was establishing in his capital a Normal School for the training of teachers to which young men from the other States of Central America were welcome. Three years before the first Normal School was opened in Massachusetts in the year 1839, President Galvez was announcing to his people that, supported by a vote of the Assembly, he was requiring that all officers in the army must attend this Normal School, and adding, for good measure, the information that he had decreed that no man without his certificate as a primary school teacher was eligible for promotion in the army.

No story of gallant effort followed by failure is more sad than that of the work of the men of high ideals who started the Central American republics on their way following the Declaration of Independence of 1821. The problems which confronted them were so great that only a miracle could have brought success. Yet they planned hopefully and moved on courageously in the intervals of civil wars which tore down as fast as they built. Of them all none left a finer record of accomplishment than this calm, strong, honorable Guatemalan statesman. A man who makes education of the people one of his chief aims can never wholly fail, for education makes its mark on the persons who are taught, even if within a few years the school system under which they were trained is swept away.

HIS BACKGROUND

Mariano Galvez, born in Guatemala in 1794, was one of the fortunate youths who went to school and university, receiving his degrees in law and letters. With Delgado, Valle, and Simeon Canas he shared in the background of learning and culture which the Spanish colonial city gave. From those student days he came out with a deep faith in popular education.

That was part of the Liberal creed in those years when the break came with Spain in 1821, and the constitution of the federated republics was adopted. Along with the abolition of slavery came enthusiasm for improving the condition of the common people. Schools were started in the towns, with government officials teaching when no other teachers were ready, while military men taught the rudiments of reading and writing and arithmetic to the

MARIANO GALVEZ
1794 - 1862

Indian soldiers in their companies. The aim was to make education a State matter, instead of having it wholly in connection with the Church and thus under the control of the priests, who could persuade the superstitious natives to almost any belief. When the civil war between the two parties was ended by Morazán's victory, the Liberal leaders took strong measures against the Roman Church, declaring that it was using its power and property to restore the rule of Spain. This was the time when the religious orders were banished and their property taken, and the leaders of the State promptly turned their buildings in one town and another into model prisons and hospitals and schools.

BECOMES PRESIDENT IN 1831

To Morazán was left the carrying on of the general plans for Central America, to Galvez, the effort to improve conditions in Guatemala. He was a practical man, as well as an idealist. Poverty was the greatest enemy to progress. Then as now the greater part of the population was Indian. President Galvez did all that he could to further agriculture, encouraging the raising of crops on the small farms for the feeding of the people and looking toward the development of agriculture in a large way in order to have exports. Spain had discouraged trade except with its own merchants. The new governments began to open their ports and welcome trade. New ports, one on the Atlantic and one on the Pacific, were opened, and new roads built to connect the different districts. There were even colonization projects for the northern unoccupied regions.

But the President's chief interest was education. He saw clearly that the new forms of government could never succeed with an ignorant people. Spain had not wished the common people educated, and the result was a backward race intellectually. Galvez increased the number of primary schools even beyond those started in the first months of the new government back in 1822 and 1824. He broadened the course of study to include history, geography, physics and natural science. Many of the ideas came from the United States, brought by Liberal exiles who had fled in the years between 1826 and 1829 and now returned from their stay in the northern republic. The Spanish and the English methods of education were thus brought together to good purpose.

EDUCATION FOR ALL

Galvez was elected President in 1831. The starting of the Normal School was one of his first acts; the purchase of a printing press the next. He wished to have new courses of study introduced and saw that he must have books and pamphlets which could be scattered far and wide showing methods of teaching as well as instructing in courses of study. It was in his message of 1836 that he made the oft-quoted statement: "The printing press acquired for public use is, in my opinion, the best means of spreading knowledge. . . . The city of Guatemala is today the center of that learning which is to be broadcast throughout the Republic."

In the same message he told how the soldiers were being educated in their barracks. They must be taught to be good citizens as well as to be soldiers in an army. "The State's three most urgent needs, as far as the army is concerned, have been satisfied: organization, discipline, and ethical training," he declared. "The barracks are now schoolhouses." At the same time he was opening an Academy of Studies, to replace the colonial University, and supplying it with a library of 15,000 volumes. He was determined that Guatemalans, from the primary schools to the colleges, should have the best education possible in that day.

There was need for a new tax system to distribute more widely the necessary payments, and he and his Assembly planned it boldly. The Church could no longer have its tenth of all money raised; and the right to trade was given to those who wished it. "Before independence," he said, "the land was owned by a few families who used their influence for personal profit; the rest of the population was composed of miserable masses, who never imagined the day would come when their condition would be the same as that of the men whose fortune dazzled them. Now, since there are no special privileges and all are subject to the same conditions, there are no great capitalists, but property ownership has increased, divided among thousands of individuals. . . . *A small clique formerly had everything and was everything, and the people were nothing; now whatever is not of the people is nothing."*

Galvez did not want a second term in office. The Liberal party was not united; the Central American Federation was going to pieces; the Republics were disagreeing, and small armies were moving across the borders. He refused reëlection once, and the Congress reëlected him. Again he declared he would not continue. The one-man rule which was to be the custom in Central America was not to his liking. He sought to "leave a chair in which no one man can do good for long."

REACTION

His prophecy of this second term, which he finally accepted, was all too true. In 1836 the terrible cholera epidemic came, and the priests found in it the chance to turn the Indians against the government. Galvez had moved too fast, as did all the leaders of the Liberal, progressive party. They had tried to put in reforms in a few brief years which would take decades in any country, especially one with an untrained people and great poverty. There were divisions in his party, which was jealous of his leadership as it was of Morazán's. In 1838 the Indian leader Carrera made his wild entry into Guatemala City. General Morazán drove him and his hordes back into the mountains, but only for a time. Soon he was back, to rule as dictator for nearly thirty years. The reforms which Galvez had started were all wiped out, and the country was under Conservative rule until the victory of Barrios in 1871 brought in a man who undertook many similar reforms with a strong hand and managed in that later day to put them through.

Galvez retired to Mexico where he practised law for more than twenty years, until his death in 1862. But when the Government of Guatemala erected its fine building for the National University in this twentieth century, it remembered the patriot who founded it as an Academy of Studies and perpetuated his name there. So a republic honors the men who were far in advance of their time, for theirs was the vision of the future which a half-century of civil wars could delay but not destroy.

MORA, COSTA RICA'S NATIONAL HERO

MORA, COSTA RICA'S NATIONAL HERO

A man whom Central Americans hold in honor
for his defense of their territory against our
North American freebooter, William Walker.

IT is always well for any of us to see ourselves as others
see us; and we of the United States can never have a
better opportunity of getting a new and somewhat unwelcome look at ourselves than by reading the story of
Juan Rafael Mora, who won his title to fame as Costa
Rica's chosen national hero by putting up a fight against
a mild-mannered Tennesseean who felt it his duty to extend the territory of the United States and bring deliver-
ance to "oppressed peoples" in Central America.

It is a curious tale, an almost unbelievable one, this
story of William Walker, the "Gray-eyed Man of Destiny," who led an expedition from California in the 1850's,
worried half a dozen governments, our own included,
became President of Nicaragua, and dreamed of a vast
slave-holding empire from Mason and Dixon's Line
southward to Panama. We dismiss it in our histories with
a page or two because he failed. But we forget that he
might not have failed. We smile over the days when an

American citizen, a doctor-lawyer-editor, a person with no military training, could sally forth with a company of kindred spirits and try to acquire territory for himself and his country according to his personal desires and ideas. But south of the San Juan River, which was in 1850 the boundary between Nicaragua and Costa Rica and also the coveted entrance to the Nicaraguan canal route, the Costa Ricans do not dismiss the matter so lightly. They and other Central Americans with them, remember with pride and some bitterness the defence which General Mora and his troops were forced to put up against these adventurers. To them this struggle is a cherished episode in their successful insistence for more than a hundred years on their national independence and sovereignty; and if we were in their places, we should feel as they do.

So it is good for us to lay our United States histories aside and start to unravel the tale from the Costa Rican end, and when we have come to know Mora in his home country, we may look with different eyes on this famous struggle.

I.

HIS BOYHOOD AND YOUTH

Juan Rafael Mora was a native of San José, the present capital of this southernmost of the Central American republics which lies just north of Panama. That city was then, as it would be now, a fortunate place in which to be born, and Juan Rafael was fortunate in his family and his

JUAN RAFAEL MORA
1814 - 1860
From the bust in the Gallery of Patriots, Washington, D. C.

position in life. He was a merchant's son, and in Costa Rica business was an honorable occupation.

Then as now Costa Rica differed from the rest of Central America by having a population which was chiefly white. The Indians of this region had fought so steadily and desperately, three hundred years before, against the Spanish conquerors who invaded their beautiful, fertile valleys, that most of them had perished. There had then come in as colonists companies of strong, hard-working people from northwest Spain, Galicians who farmed their own land and built up their own healthy civilization. Costa Rica has always had its middle class of citizens, as well as its aristocratic families and its laborers.

Juan Rafael was born on February 8, 1814, to Don Camilo Mora and Doña Benita Porras. On both sides the families were distinguished. A Juan Mora, member of another line of the family, had been the first President of the republic after it adopted its first constitution in 1825. His wise and progressive rule, which lasted for eight years, gave the government a good start, and he was recalled to high office by Francisco Morazán during his brief period of control and again by later Presidents. Don Camilo Mora was a business man who held public office in colonial days and was active in the beginning of independence after 1821.

As a schoolboy Juan was remembered as showing intelligence and keen observation. Twenty years later he was to issue clear-cut, strong proclamations, showing the benefit of his early training. At sixteen he left school to help his father in his shop in the plaza of the city, and it is pleasant to know that the customers called him *don Juanito,* expressing thus their satisfaction in his courtesy and readiness to serve them.

Those five years must have been remembered as the most happy of his youth, for when he was barely twenty-one his father died, and his hard struggle with the world began. It was found that Don Camilo's affairs were in bad shape, and Juan Rafael had to take over the care of a large family of younger brothers and sisters as well as to assume his father's debts. Creditors demanded that these be paid at once, and there was no money with which to do it. The high opinion in which the young man was held is shown by the prompt offer of a friend of the family to stand security for these obligations, with Juan's promise to work hard and make repayment as his only guarantee.

The next years developed in the young merchant the strength of character which was to win him public office in later years. He undertook the management of the family, insisting on rigid economy on the part of his brothers and sisters, and gave himself to unremitting labor. At last he was able to pay the last peso on the debts, and in the years of work toward that goal, he had become greatly interested in farming, which was then, as it is now, the most profitable occupation in this rich, semi-tropical land.

COSTA RICA IN THOSE DAYS

The American "official observer," Mr. Stephens, whose opinions of Morazán and Carrera we have quoted, visited Costa Rica in 1839 and gives us a picture of it in these years when young Mora was beginning to do business for himself.

San José is, I believe, [writes Stephens] the only city that has grown up or even improved since the independence of Central America. Under the Spanish dominion Cartago was the royal capital; but on the breaking out of revolution, the fervor of patriotism was so hot that it was resolved to abolish this memorial of colonial servitude, and establish the capital at San José. Their local advantages are perhaps equal. Cartago is nearer the Atlantic, and San José the Pacific; but they are only six leagues apart. The buildings in San José are all republican; there is not one of any grandeur or architectural beauty; and the churches are inferior to many erected by the Spaniards in the smallest villages. Nevertheless, it exhibited a development of resources and an appearance of business unusual in this lethargic country. . . .

The State of Costa Rica enjoyed at that time a degree of prosperity unequalled by any of the disjointed confederacy. At a safe distance, without wealth enough to excite cupidity, and with a large tract of wilderness to protect it against the march of an invading army, it has escaped the tumults and wars which desolated and devastated the other States.

Young Mora became especially successful in raising coffee, a crop which was only being tried out experimentally at that time but was to become the country's chief export. The official heroes of the Central American countries are political figures, like our own Washington and Lincoln, but there are other men who made their important contributions toward the prosperity of their countries. Among these is the Brazilian who in the early part of the nineteenth century brought a coffee tree from his homeland and planted it in his yard. From so small a beginning is said to have grown the country's enormous coffee culture. That man did his part for independence, too, for Costa Rica's later independence came through her coffee crop, which helped to pay the national debt and gave her citizens prosperity, as neither constitutions nor wars could have done.

AS A LEADING CITIZEN

Mora was far-sighted and progressive when he cultivated the new product and encouraged others to do the same. According to local records he was, in the year 1848, the owner of an estate that produced five thousand quintals of coffee, which was a large crop for those days. As he came more into public life, he also did everything to advertise native Costa Rican products, urging the cultivation of bananas, cacao, rice and corn, and the exploiting of valuable dyewoods and lumber and of metals from the ancient mines. He was ready to give advice, and often practical assistance, to anyone who came to him with a proposition of farming more land. He had grown up with the period of independence and was eager to see the Republic make itself independent, as its location with shores on both oceans and yet a separateness from its neighbor nations would seem to make possible.

In 1847 he was made Vice-President, and promptly showed his soldierly qualities by leading a force of soldiers to put down a revolt against the government. Yet the Mora of these days was not by choice a soldier or a fighter. He is described as being a "man of attractive appearance, medium height, broad shoulders, dark eyes, a thoughtful expression, and a gentle voice that became sonorous and firm when giving orders. He spent all the time possible with his family; his meals were frugal; he loved order, sincerity, and work. He was straight in all his affairs, and he did not tolerate crookedness in others."

Such was Juan Rafael Mora when he was elected President in 1852 and reëlected the following year on a platform of promising improvements and public works which would be of benefit to Costa Rica. It would have seemed as if he and the hundred thousand citizens of the little republic had chosen a program of progress and comparative peace.

BRITISH-AMERICAN DISPUTES

But peace was not to be had in those days in Central America. The gold rush to California had focussed attention on the narrow body of land which was all that separated the Atlantic (the Caribbean Sea) and the Pacific oceans. The United States had taken Texas from Mexico, and Great Britain was not going to forego any claims she had in Central America. The Caribbean coast had been the seat of early British settlements, logging camps and hideaways in inlets and forests for pirates and traders. At this time the stretch of territory which we call British Honduras was being held, and England was laying claim also to the strip of land along the Nicaraguan coast which was the kingdom of the Mosquito Indians. In 1850 she took possession, in the name of "His Mosquito Majesty," of the town at the mouth of the San Juan River which was the gateway of the probable route of a Nicaraguan Canal. Nicaragua protested ineffectually, and turned to the government at Washington for help. The party in power even suggested, as if it had the right to decide for itself and its neighbors, that Nicaragua, Salvador, and Honduras be admitted to the American Union. The weak little republic had small hope in those days of holding its own between the rival claims of the two great English-speaking nations to a canal route from ocean to ocean.

One can imagine President Mora and his Costa Ricans looking on while this dispute waxed hot. The United States had, as a matter of fact, no desire to acquire Central America, but it was not going to let England gain control of the canal route. The two nations were almost ready to go to war over their differences when, in 1850, the Clayton-Bulwer Treaty restored peace. There must have been intense relief in Costa Rica, which lay to the south of the San Juan River, when this treaty was signed making the canal route neutral territory for the two powers, and pledging both nations not to "occupy, or fortify, or colonize, or assume or exercise any dominion over Nicaragua, Costa Rica, the Mosquito Coast, or any part of Central America." That was a definite statement on which the little nations must have thought they could rely. But all the discussion had roused men like Mora to intense nationalism. The Costa Ricans were determined to keep their independence at any cost—and within five years there came William Walker!

II.

WILLIAM WALKER OF TENNESSEE

What of this American whose name was to be a byword of terror with which mothers all up and down the Isthmus threatened their naughty children for a generation? Even in the days when he was leading his army and serving as President of Nicaragua, he did not look the part of a "soldier of fortune," and certainly there was no sign of his future in his boyhood.

He was the son of a Scotchman, James Walker, who had immigrated to Nashville, Tennessee, in 1820, and there married Mary Norvell of Kentucky. William, the oldest of four children, was born on May 8, 1824, and went to school in Nashville, showing himself of more than average keenness of mind but restless and not willing to apply himself more than was necessary. The neighbors remembered him later as rather an effeminate boy, devoted to his invalid mother, and "as refined in his feelings as a girl." He was of small stature, never growing to be more than five and a half feet tall or coming to weigh more than one hundred pounds. Boyish sports did not attract him. No one would have dreamed of his becoming a leader of men.

The University of Nashville, from which he graduated while he was still very young, gave an excellent cultural and classical education, according to the standards of the time, and was also strong in its emphasis on moral and religious training. There were required chapel services daily, classes in the study of the Bible on Sunday, and strict rules of conduct for the students, with amusements such as dancing, theater going, and attendance at horse races forbidden. It was natural that young William should come out of this institution a silent, shy, and thoughtful youth.

His parents had hoped that he would enter the ministry, but they were ready to do everything to further his wishes when he chose medicine as a profession. After studying for a time with the leading physician of the city, he went to the University of Pennsylvania, from which he received the degree of M.D. when he was only nineteen years old, and then abroad for two years, studying in Paris for a first year and then traveling from one city of Europe to another, widening his knowledge of the world and gaining

WILLIAM WALKER

a convenient familiarity with the French, German, and Italian languages.

Thus equipped, he returned to his native city with every opportunity to become a distinguished surgeon, but the restless spirit which had begun to show itself in his school days led him to abandon medicine and take up the study of law. In this calling he went far enough to be admitted to the bar in the city of New Orleans, but failure to make a good living in his first practice of law turned him to journalism. He became one of the editors of the New Orleans *Crescent,* and was making a name for himself by his writings on its editorial page when, in 1849, the paper failed, leaving the young doctor-lawyer-editor under the necessity of deciding what he would do next.

At this time one of the terrible yellow fever epidemics which swept Southern ports in those days visited New Orleans, and to the horror of the experience there was added for young Walker the personal shock of the death of the young lady whom he was to marry. Friends declared that this sorrow changed him greatly. He was very melancholy, and showed also from that time on what one of them described as "a daring ambition and a reckless disregard of life."

ON TO CALIFORNIA

For a restless and reckless young American of the year 1849 there was one answer—California with its gold rush. Walker made the long journey across the continent to the western coast, and settled in San Francisco early in the year 1850, becoming a member of the San Francisco *Daily Herald*. His recklessness took the form of complete frankness in what he wrote. His editorials concerning the tolerance of crime by courts and judges in the pioneer town were so critical that he was arrested for libel and thrown into prison. At large he had been practically unknown; in prison he became a martyr and a hero. The issue of free speech was raised; citizens flocked to his defense; mass meetings were held at which his release was demanded. He was soon released, but when the excitement died down, he was restless again, and moved on to Marysville, a fast-growing pioneer town. There he practised law for a couple of years, but without finding any real satisfaction for his ambition.

HE TURNS TO FILIBUSTERING

The word "filibuster," which came into common use at that time, comes from the Dutch word for "freebooter." Webster in his dictionary uses Walker as an example of its usage. "A filibuster," he writes, "is a freebooter or soldier-of-fortune who aids in a revolution in a foreign country in order to enrich himself; first applied to buccaneers in the West Indies, who preyed on the Spanish commerce to South America, and later to such adventurers as followed Lopez to Cuba, and Walker to Nicaragua in their expeditions of conquest."

If we are to be fair to Walker, as well as to our Costa

Rican hero Mora as his opponent, we must catch a little of the spirit of American pioneer life at that time. For seventy-five years the American frontier had been moving west. Now it had come to the ocean's edge. There were only two ways for the country to expand, northward into Canada, or southward into the region which had been part of the Spanish empire until thirty years earlier and was still unsettled in its political life.

Moreover, there was a fixed idea that America *must* expand. The Mexican War was just over, with Texas a newly acquired part of the United States. Men of those days could not grasp the idea that the boundaries of the United States might be already fixed. They had a curious and attractive theory of our "manifest destiny," a theory which it is interesting to recall at this moment when it is being expounded by nations on other continents as their aim.

Laurence Greene, Walker's latest biographer, has unearthed in a San Francisco volume of the year 1855 a naive and astonishing statement of this "manifest destiny" theory.

It is the fate of America ever to go ahead, [say its authors]. She is like the rod of Aaron that became a serpent and swallowed up the other rods. So will America conquer or annex all lands. That is her "manifest destiny."

Only give her time for the process. To swallow up every few years a province as large as most European kingdoms is her present rate of progress. Sometimes she

purchases the mighty morsel; sometimes she forms it out
of waste territory by the natural increase of her own people; sometimes she "annexes" and sometimes she con-
quers it.

With a cynicism which is also not unfamiliar in our
own time, the authors continue that another means of
acquiring such territory may be by the efforts of filibusters,
"who steal and fight gratuitously for their own fast-fol-
lowing Uncle Sam."

THE MEXICAN ADVENTURE

Such a philosophy was current among practical men in
every class of society, and nowhere more so than among
the adventurers who had been drawn to California from
every quarter of the world by the lure of gold. William
Walker had attracted attention by his editorial writings.
He was an earnest soul, more than ready to believe that
there was a "manifest destiny" for him as well as for his
nation. When the call came from a group of kindred
spirits to lead them in an expedition for acquiring land
and colonizing Indian-occupied mining regions in Lower
California, which was the property of Mexico, he was
eager to go. The Indians who worked the mines were
being oppressed, according to his explanation; the land
was undeveloped; it was his mission to colonize this region of Sonora and give it "independence."

The story of that unsuccessful expedition does not belong in this chronicle, save as it shows a Walker full of

grandiose schemes, who went about setting up a "Republic of Lower California," issued solemn proclamations establishing its territorial bounds, and declared himself its President at a moment when, with a small fighting force under his command, he was still endeavoring to make the conquest. The little company of fighters performed bold deeds and won some small successes, but they were finally forced to make their defeated way back to California. The taste for foreign adventure and military achievement had, however, been awakened in him, and he was eager for more of it.

When the members of the Sonora expedition straggled back into California, they found that a change had come in the official attitude to filibustering. The government had not been paying much attention to it. Now the Secretary of War, Jefferson Davis, had sent out from Washington a new commander of the Department of the Pacific with instructions to prosecute offenders who had designs on Mexican territory or intended any filibustering attempt. The commander's duty was to "maintain the nation's obligations by preventing unlawful expeditions against the territories of foreign powers." The instructions went further. "Confidence is felt," the Secretary of War wrote, "that you will, to the utmost of your ability, use all proper means to detect the fitting out of armed expeditions against countries with which the United States are at peace."

Two companions of Walker, returning to California

in advance of him, were brought before the courts and given heavy fines. Walker, likewise arrested and brought to trial, was acquitted by a friendly jury who followed the obvious wish of the presiding judge to have the filibuster's escapade treated lightly. One might have thought that a mandate against filibustering would give him pause. But he seems to have been more than ready when a newly arrived New Englander, Byron Cole by name, approached him with a scheme for colonization and conquest in Nicaragua.

NICARAGUAN INVITATION

The project which Byron Cole put forth was of just the sort to appeal to Walker, who was giving up with the utmost reluctance his plans for colonizing in Sonora. Cole had chosen to come to California by the route across the Isthmus instead of by the long overland trip across the continent, and he had come through Nicaragua instead of Panama. The beauties of Nicaragua and its possibilities for development had made a deep impression on him, and he had seen, as did all travelers of that time, how hopeless was its condition if the factional strife between its two political parties continued.

In spite of its natural advantages Nicaragua had made little advance since the winning of independence. There was bitter enmity between its two leading cities, Granada, center for the aristocratic party, the conservatives or Legitimists, as they were called here, and León, the home of the Liberals. For twenty years there had been such constant strife that the villages and towns of the country had lost much of their male population in battle. The fields were uncultivated. The walls of the cities, and even of the churches and the homes, were riddled with bullet holes which told to the passing traveler the tale of the constant warfare. Nor were Nicaraguans alone involved in the rivalry. Party lines were stronger than national lines in the weaker republics, and it was the custom for any defeated official to slip across the border into the next State and there win support and perhaps military help for his return to power.

Such a man was Castellon, a Liberal of the city of León, who had failed to win the presidency and was proceeding to lay siege to his rival's city of Granada, where the new government was attempting to function. It is said that in the two years before Walker came to Nicaragua there had been six successive presidents. Castellon happened to be out of office instead of in, and did not at all like his position. Byron Cole's idea was to take advantage of these Nicaraguan quarrels and get a foothold for developing the rich, impoverished country. Castellon was only too pleased with the suggestion that three hundred Americans might be brought to the republic to fight for him, especially when Cole held out the hope that the "renowned Walker" might be their leader.

The offer which Castellon made was of salaries for each soldier and a large grant of land at the close of the campaign. When Walker heard the proposal, he knew that by the new United States law it was illegal. But his training in the law came to his aid. He sent Cole back to Nicaragua to obtain from Castellon a "contract of colonization." This document, which was shortly brought back, permitted Walker to enlist in California not soldiers but "colonists" to the number of three hundred, with the provision that these men should, on arrival, become citizens of Nicaragua, and also—note the phrase!—"have forever the privilege of bearing arms." The adventurers could sail from the California port with all their rifles, revolvers, and bowie knives because they were "colonists," and the Nicaraguans could not deprive them of these useful weapons. It was a barefaced scheme, but it did not break the law.

ANOTHER AMERICAN IN NICARAGUA

In order to understand how such a plan of entering and exploiting the Central American country could be considered, it is well to follow our custom of stopping for a moment to "interview" a traveler of the time. An American mining engineer, Mr. William V. Wells, went to Honduras in 1854 with the purpose of obtaining gold-mining privileges from that government. The idea had originated with a New York merchant, but the papers and documents connected with the enterprise had found their way to California, where, as Mr. Wells says in his published journal, "the broad liberality and eager spirit of adventure at that date seemed to offer a more genial soil for the inception of such projects." Byron Cole and William Walker were not the only ones to look with longing eyes at the undeveloped resources of their southern neighbors.

In the course of his journeyings Mr. Wells went to Nicaragua and gives this picture of the state of that country which Walker and his men were so soon to enter. "León in 1854, like every other Nicaraguan city, presented a sorry spectacle. In fact, the town is falling to decay, and every species of improvement has long since ceased. With the frantic revolutions which have successively swept over the country, the finest residences of the old Spanish families have been burned or torn down, until now, though the first city of the republic, it is but the ghost of its former self. I passed through one street lined on either side with ruined arches and walls, the whole overgrown with massive verdure and resembling the relics of some aboriginal race. In 1823 this part of the city, comprising nearly two thousand houses, was destroyed by fire. The gardens, formerly extending back from the streets, are now choked with weeds and ruins. I know of nothing sadder than the apparent certainty with which these people seem to be hurrying themselves out of political existence."

Mr. Wells goes on to tell of the election disputed by Castellon and the defeated candidate's intention of moving on Granada, with such help as he could get in neighboring countries, and remarks on the ancient feud existing between the rival cities, "in which families, intermarried, have become estranged, and bitter jealousies have given rise to incessant wars."

He adds the information that León contained about 15,000 inhabitants, among whom were many of the most illustrious families in Central America. "There are several public buildings with some pretensions to elegance. Its churches are more numerous and larger than those of any other Central American city excepting Guatemala." He was particularly impressed by the cathedral, the interior of which had all the impressive grandeur of the European cathedrals. "Its roof has served as a fortress in times of siege, and no better evidence is wanting of the fearful struggles which have taken place around it than the thousands of bullet marks scarring its venerable walls."

It is a sad picture of the proud city of the early years of independence. This was what Walker and the recruits whom he was then assembling were to see when they arrived the following year.

THE "IMMORTALS"

There was probably no place in the world save California where such a company could have been recruited so readily. He did not get the permitted three hundred. A first success must be achieved before so many could be won to the scheme, and there was a shortage of funds. But a small sum of money was raised and a leaky old vessel, the *Vesta,* purchased and put in repair. Innumerable difficulties threatened the attempt at every step, among them a personal duel which Walker fought and in which he received a serious wound in his foot, and also the attachment of the vessel by the sheriff on the eve of its intended sailing for payment of the previous owner's debts. This last obstacle was overcome by setting sail with the sheriff in the cabin and offering him either handcuffs and a voyage to Nicaragua or the chance to go ashore on a small returning boat. He naturally chose the latter alternative, and the *Vesta* proceeded on its slow way with fifty-eight men aboard, having sailed out of Sacramento harbor on May 4, 1855.

The "Immortals," as they were to be called, were a picturesque and varied crowd of would-be fighters. There were experienced soldiers who had fought in the Mexican War or been with Lopez on a similar filibustering expedition to Cuba. Some of the men had accompanied Walker on the Sonora enterprise and were ready to follow wherever he led. A surgeon of the party had lately returned from an unsuccessful search in the Cocos Islands for buried treasure. Others were miners, storekeepers, and other emigrants to California who had not found the fortunes they had anticipated and were ready to try again, perhaps with an excellent reason for getting out of the towns where they had run up debts or bad records. They were a wild, independent group for any man to handle, but the smooth-spoken, fiery little Tennesseean was equal to the task.

WALKER BECOMES THE 'GRAY-EYED MAN OF DESTINY'

Men who met Walker could never quite believe that the small, unprepossessing, quiet man was the formidable leader of whom they had heard. At this time his appearance had not changed greatly from his student days, and he certainly did not look the part of a military chieftain.

A man who saw him during the Mexican campaign describes him as below medium height, very slim, hardly weighing more than one hundred pounds. He goes on to say: "His hair was light and towy, while his almost white eyebrows and lashes concealed a seemingly pupilless gray, cold eye. . . . His dress was scarcely less remarkable than his person. His head was surmounted by a huge white fur hat, whose long knap waved with the breeze, which, together with a very ill-made, short-waisted blue coat, with gilt buttons, and a pair of greasy, strapless pantaloons, made up the ensemble of as unprepossessing-looking a person as one would meet in a day's walk. . . . But anyone who estimated Mr. Walker by his personal appearance made a great mistake. Extremely taciturn, he would sit for an hour in company without opening his lips; but once interested he arrested your attention with the first word he uttered, and as he proceeded, you felt convinced that he was no ordinary person."

One of his young soldiers gives us another picture, one more in keeping with the views of his devoted followers.

"His body," he says, "was strong, and his vital energy surprisingly great. The expression of his countenance was frank and open, and heightened by the absence of beard of any kind. His aggressive and determined character was plainly indicated by his aquiline nose, while his eyes, from which came his sobriquet, 'Gray-eyed Man of Destiny,' were keen in their scrutiny and almost hypnotic in their power. A woman's voice was scarcely softer than Walker's, and so imperturbable was he that his praise of a valorous deed or his announcement of a death sentence were equally calm in tone and deliberate in enunciation. Though affable in intercourse, he suppressed his emotions, whether of joy or sadness, and did not permit himself to be startled by surprise. . . . I cannot recall ever having seen him smile. But with all his placidity of voice and demeanor, men leaped eagerly into the very cannon's mouth to obey his commands."

The "intense, brilliant, blue-gray eyes" were the feature most noticed by those who met him. The dark-skinned native peoples were almost ready to worship him, for there was an ancient tradition that a gray-eyed white man from afar would come to rule over them. Joaquin Miller, the California poet, who was his intimate friend, speaks of him as "most impressive on the firing line . . . with his gray eyes expanding and glittering like broken steel with rage of battle."

III.

STRANGE HAPPENINGS

There are strange pictures all along the way in this curious story of North Americans battling in the Central American republic.

There is the picture of their arrival and of their being reviewed by Castellon in the public square in the city of León, while the wondering natives looked on. They were such a contrast to the local soldiery, these tall, bearded, self-confident men in their familiar California pioneer costume of cotton breeches, miners' boots, flannel shirts in blue, gray or red, with wide-brimmed felt hats. It was not a uniform, and yet it had the effect of being one. They stood before the Nicaraguan President with easy uncon-cern, every man equipped with at least two of the weap-ons they had brought with them, the revolvers, rifles, and bowie knives. He named them the "American phalanx," declared them Nicaraguan citizens, made Walker a colo-nel, and sent him out with orders to capture one of the Legitimist towns for him. They were fifty-five against five hundred, but they rendered good account of them-selves, fighting a bloody battle in which many Nicara-guans were wounded and killed, and a proper fear of the newcomers was instilled into the minds of the natives.

The tales of "battle, murder, and sudden death," of dis-covered treachery, of executions by Walker, and slowly growing fear on the part of his own men and the Legitimist enemy, belong to the past and need not be revived here. But there are pictures which remain. In October Walker achieved the bold stroke of surprising the garrison at Granada and taking the city.

That won him fame in all Central America and in the United States, where volunteers crowded every southern-sailing boat to join his army. He won the gratitude of Granadans by forbidding his men to plunder the city, and they marveled at the sudden peace which descended when the fair-skinned, bearded soldiers patrolled the streets. There is a tale of the appearance of three recruits with drums and fife who paraded through the plaza playing "Yankee Doodle" and "Hail Columbia," and of Colonel Walker's coming out from his quarters to speak to the marching men who had fallen in behind them and saying: "Fellow citizens and soldiers, this is, perhaps, the first time such music has been heard on the plaza of Granada; let us hope that it may be heard through future ages!"

A year later his troops were to evacuate the city, leaving it in ruins, with hardly one stone upon another, and the significant sign erected, "Here was Granada." But now he was in power and in favor with the people.

There were those who shared Walker's feeling of the great benefit which was to be conferred on this country by the coming in of the Americans. The phrases used are strongly reminiscent of the words of conquerors and dictators in this following century. "A new civilization is about to be engrafted upon the older and decadent one," says one interpreter of the undertaking. But there were also those who appreciated the culture of the Nicaraguan people of Spanish descent who were battling with these problems of political strife and native ignorance and superstition. A young soldier reports the social aristocracy of Nicaragua as possessing the wealth and beauty of Old Spain.

> In the larger cities of Nicaragua [says J. C. Jamison] were families that preserved the aristocratic customs and traditions of their Spanish ancestors. They possessed wealth and lived in luxury. Frequently their sons and daughters were educated at the universities and the convents of Europe, and in this way exclusive Nicaraguan society maintained an elegance and brilliancy, a delicacy and refinement, that found expression in the grace of its women and the gallantry of its men.

A weekly newspaper was printed in English and Spanish, a propaganda sheet of the "new order." In one of its early issues the tradition of the prophecy of the coming of a "Gray-eyed Man" was related, with an account of the coming of a delegation of Indians to the city and their offering of thanks to Colonel Walker for their "liberation from oppression and for the present state of quiet of the country."

MORA PREPARES FOR WAR

The peoples of the other Central American republics were watching events in this between-oceans region. They had seen it becoming, within the previous five or six years, a source of strife between British and Americans because of its being an easy bridge between the Caribbean and the Pacific. There was jealousy of its new prominence and suspicion of the entrance of foreigners into its affairs. Information as to Walker's doings came from Legitimists, members of the opposing party, who sought refuge in the neighbor republics of Honduras to the north and Costa Rica to the south, where President Mora was beginning his second term of office as head of a Legitimist, or Conservative, government.

To these republics Walker extended invitations for friendship through the new provisional President of Nicaragua, whom he had had chosen. These communications expressed the desire for peace and urged friendship between the republics. The attitude toward this move in each republic was according to the political party then in power. Most of them sent no official response, but El Salvador was inclined to approve of the success of their party, the Liberals or Democrats. There were even leaders in both El Salvador and Honduras who saw in William Walker a successor to their honored Francisco Morazán, who, we remember, had stood always for a union of the republics. This was entirely in accord with Walker's own idea of his mission.

Costa Rica, under Mora, would have none of such plans. In November Mora issued a public proclamation against the Americans. The peace of his country was endangered, he declared. To the neighbor State have come a "band of adventurers, the scum of all peoples, condemned by the judiciary of the American Union," who would next be planning to invade Costa Rica.

"Is it necessary," he asks, "to paint the terrible evils which may result from our coolly awaiting so barbarous an invasion? No, you understand them. You know well what may be expected of a horde of adventurers fleeing from their fatherland. You know your duty.

"Be alert, then, Costa Ricans! Do not halt your noble labors, but make ready your arms!"

This was the beginning of the open Central American opposition to Walker and his government which was to grow as the months went on. Walker made every effort to conciliate the Costa Rican President, sending friendly messages to him and finally despatching a delegation, which was turned back at the border.

It has been easy for North Americans to paint a black picture of President Mora. "An unswerving aristocrat, cruel adversary, skilled politician and violent nationalist," Laurence Greene calls him. But as one follows the course of this merchant-President through these months, one can but feel some sympathy with his attitude. The Costa Rican minister at Washington, his representative, was equally bitter. In a communication to our government in December he asserts that Walker's undertaking was "a great crime, complex and multiform, which was hatched and set on foot within the territory of the United States and continued without interruption in a foreign land by North American citizens, with means and assistance and to a certain extent with the moral force of the nation, against the existence of peaceable and friendly States." To this accusation he adds the significant words, "If the adventurers are disowned by the government today, they hope, not without cause, to be received with open arms tomorrow, arrayed in holiday attire for annexation, and to be exalted, their booty being legitimatized."

It was true that no effort was being made to halt the Nicaraguan enterprise, even though President Pierce was giving it no official approval. By the winter of 1856 Walker's agents were advertising openly for emigrants, as the Costa Rican minister doubtless informed President Mora. The advertisements are interesting. One in the *New York Herald* is a masterly piece of Yankee understatement.

Wanted.—Ten or fifteen young men to go a short distance out of the city. Single men preferred. Apply at 347 Broadway, corner of Leonard Street, room 12, between hours of ten and four. Passage paid.

In New Orleans the announcement was more frank.

Nicaragua.—The Government of Nicaragua is desirous of having its land settled and cultivated by an industrious class of people, and offers as an inducement to emigrants a donation of Two Hundred and Fifty Acres of Land for single persons, and One Hundred Acres addition to persons of family. Steamers leave New Orleans for San Juan on the 11th and 29th of each month. The fare is now reduced to less than half the former rates. The undersigned will be happy to give information to those who are desirous of emigrating. Thos. F. Fisher, 16 Royal St.

They were harmless-appearing statements, but there were few who did not know that when the colonists arrived, they were likely to spend a period in Walker's army before they settled on their land.

In February of 1856 Mora called his Congress together and gained their authority to take up arms against the Americans. He was careful to state that this move was not against Nicaragua, but for it, his purpose being the defense of the republic from these invaders and the expulsion of the North Americans from all the territory of Central America. *"Guerra solo a los filibusteros!"* ("War only on the filibusters!") was his word as he issued a call for an army, levied a war tax, and prepared for action. President Rivas of Nicaragua promptly declared war on Costa Rica, and in March the Costa Rican army was on the way.

CORNELIUS VANDERBILT AND HIS TRANSIT COMPANY

President Mora was to have two allies in his fight against Walker, the powerful American financier, Cornelius Vanderbilt, who had been transporting gold seekers across the Isthmus by a Nicaraguan route since 1850, and British interests, which looked with strong disapproval

THE VOLCANO AGUA

Central America abounds in volcanoes, few of which are now active. It was in valleys rich in volcanic
ash that coffee was first successfully grown.

on the American seizure of this valuable inter-oceanic route. Looking back on the entire episode, with all the secret letters and state papers now in hand as evidence, historians find every move complicated by the British-American contest for power. Before war was declared, Walker had taken from a steamer bound for Costa Rica a bag of mail with letters which revealed that Mora was corresponding with his Consul General in London over British shipment of arms to the Costa Ricans. "When I was telling Lord Clarendon that Costa Rica already had an army of 800 men on the frontier of Nicaragua," wrote this Costa Rican official to his home government, "he was very much pleased and said 'that was a right step,' and I am persuaded that my having made that insinuation is one of the reasons for giving us the muskets." The letter ended with a comment that though the government of the United States was appearing to censure the American Minister to Nicaragua for his acceptance of the Walker government, the United States would in a short time recognize that government.

Walker had made his great mistake, however, in antagonizing Commodore Vanderbilt. That shrewd financier had early perceived the opportunity in Nicaragua's water system of two lakes and a river which nearly spanned the Isthmus. Back in Spanish times vessels had used this route, going up the San Juan River into Lake Nicaragua, along its hundred miles and across a narrow separating strip of land to Lake Managua, and out by land to the

Pacific. The gold seekers who took the Panama route for California had to cross the Isthmus by muleback. Vanderbilt got permission to put steamships on Lake Nicaragua, organized a Transit Company, and did a thriving business carrying travelers across the Isthmus, saving two days over his Panama rivals in the length of the journey to California.

THE TRIP ACROSS THE ISTHMUS

The story of that undertaking is a saga of American enterprise. Vanderbilt had started out with the idea of a Nicaraguan canal and had secured a charter from the government for a right of way through Nicaraguan territory and the exclusive right to build a canal. He had interested British financiers in the proposition and prepared to launch it if surveys indicated that such a canal could be built. When the difficulties proved too great, he changed his plans to this transportation scheme, organizing a "Transit Company," which was safeguarded against rivals by having in its charter a monopoly, granted by the Nicaraguan government, of navigating the waters of the State by steam. With this permission he was ready to go into business.

He put a couple of small steamboats on the river that led from the Caribbean to Lake Nicaragua, and a couple of bigger boats on the great lake, sending steamers around Cape Horn to the Pacific to be ready to carry the passengers from the Isthmus to California. From Virgin Bay,

on the farther side of Lake Nicaragua it was a dozen or
more miles to the Pacific port where these ocean steamers could be boarded. At first this trip had to be made by
muleback over a rough path. But by the year 1854, the
year before Walker came to Nicaragua, a macadam road
had been completed and stagecoaches imported. Travelers crossed the lake in steamers with comfortable state-
rooms, and then entered stagecoaches, painted patrioti-
cally in the Nicaraguan colors, blue and white, which were
drawn by four mules along the smooth roadway to the
coast. They returned home to tell of the beauties of the
scenery of Nicaragua and of the impressive sight of lines
of twenty-five such coaches starting out after the arrival
of a boat and proceeding in a single line, with wagons
filled with baggage following.

Twenty-five thousand persons are said to have made
that trip during the rush years of travel, two thousand going in a single month. The fare from New York to San
Francisco on a Vanderbilt ticket was reduced to three
hundred dollars, in order to compete with the six-hun-
dred dollar fare that was charged on the Panama route
before the competition began. Byron Cole had come by
that route; Nicaragua had been made known by that
route:—and William Walker in his egotism and the first
months of his success, after the occupation of the city of
Granada, made enemies of Vanderbilt and his associates by
having his Nicaraguan government revoke the Transit
Company's charter until there should be an investigation

to determine whether they were paying their promised share of profits into the republic's treasury!

PUBLIC OPINION

There were reasons for his act, as there were always wheels within wheels in the Central American transactions of this period. The Costa Rican envoys in the United States had made so much protest against the free transportation of filibusters who responded to the advertisements that President Pierce had been forced to take notice of the Walker activities. He issued a proclamation warning all persons against taking any part in the fitting out of such expeditions, and had every Isthmus-bound ship searched. But he might as well have tried to stop the flowing of a stream with a few pieces of paper. A seventeen-year-old boy when seized and questioned as to why he was going to Nicaragua declared in the district attorney's office, "For fun," and no amount of questioning could extract any further information. How could the authorities say that these passengers were not going on to California? Jealous rivals of the Transit Company managed to throw all the blame upon its shoulders, and Walker felt obliged to grant a charter to another company headed by men who had aided him greatly in gaining recruits in New York and elsewhere.

The news of Vanderbilt's loss of his charter brought comments in the New York newspapers which show how popular Walker's acts in virtually taking over the Nicaraguan government were in the United States. In the *New York Herald* in the month when Mora and his troops were preparing to march into Nicaragua there was an editorial stating that the great mass of the American people sympathized deeply with Walker's government. They "will regret to find," it continues "that its gallant head has perilled its hitherto bright prospects."

Vanderbilt withdrew at once his ocean steamers, cutting off supplies for the filibusters. President Mora saw in this confusion a chance for Costa Rica to revive an old claim to the territory on either side of the San Juan River and so keep the route across the Isthmus in the hands of Central Americans instead of foreigners. He accompanied his declaration of war with an announcement that, since the Transit Company's steamers were carrying "bandits," he was ordering a stoppage of traffic on both river and lake. When the news of this high-handed act came to the Secretary of State in Washington, he naturally declined to recognize it. As it happened, there were no steamers moving in these troubled times. So the paper blockade amounted to nothing, but it shows the lengths to which President Mora was willing to go.

THE FIRST FIGHTING—AND A COSTA RICAN HERO

Walker and his army were surprised by President Mora's sudden move against them. He followed his declaration of war by taking command personally of the army, and came quickly across jungles and marshes and swamps and through tropical forests to make the attack. One of the fierce early battles was at the town of Rivas. The Costa Ricans far outnumbered the small Walker force, who were caught within the town. They fought desperately, and hours went by with the Costa Rican army being raked by the shots poured from their guns. Then came a brave act which has made the battle famous in Costa Rican annals.

The Walker men had taken refuge in a large inn on the plaza, and no attacks could dislodge them. The General called for a volunteer to set fire to the roof. A young mulatto private, a small, slight fellow, stepped forward. He showed that he knew the attempt meant almost certain death by asking his companions not to forget his old mother. Seizing a flaming torch, he ran forward and pushed it under the eaves of the roof. A rain of shots followed him, and a bullet hit his right arm and disabled it. He caught the flaming stick in his left hand and continued to thrust it up into the eaves until he was shot down. The flames spread over the roof, and as it fell in, the besieged men rushed forth to be met by the Costa Ricans.

A monument stands in Costa Rica today portraying Juan Santamaria in the act of running eagerly forward with his torch uplifted. No deed of the unhappy war has been so long remembered as that willing sacrifice.

General Mora won the town, though with heavy losses, but the survivors among Walker's men managed to make their way out under cover of darkness without having their escape discovered by their besiegers. Neither side followed up the battle with further action. It would have been expected that General Mora would march forward and continue his attacks, but he stayed on in the town, and a more terrible enemy than Walker's fighting men came upon his army. Cholera appeared and spread fast among the men. The Costa Rican forces suffered heavily, and their commander was forced to order them to retreat. The plague followed them back to their homes, where the President had to call in doctors to do their utmost to combat it. In spite of their efforts ten thousand persons died before it was stamped out.

THE CONFLICT CONTINUES

It is not the custom of Central Americans, and certainly not of North Americans, to dwell on the details of fighting long past. The political moves are longer remembered. Walker found his Nicaraguan President unsatisfactory and was himself elected to the position in June of that year. In July he took office with an inauguration ceremony in the plaza of Granada. By this time he knew that the other republics were against him, and he represented himself in his address as defending the dignity and sovereignty of Nicaragua against them and against the world.

The amazing part of the story is the intense interest of Americans in the United States in the affairs in Central

America. There were two reasons for this, the first, an attitude of resentment against Great Britain with a desire to prevent any increase of British power on the Isthmus, and the second, the division between North and South which was coming to open expression. Walker played up to this by abolishing, as soon as he came to the Presidency, the federal decree won so many years ago in the constitutional convention which forbade slavery. For the development of the country which he planned, he felt that African labor was needed. That act won for him the sympathy of the South, as the belief grew that he intended to establish in Central America one or more slaveholding States, to be joined closely with those of the United States.

Still it is almost unbelievable to find the question of recognition of the Walker regime in Nicaragua becoming an issue of the Presidential campaign in 1856, with President Pierce recognizing the new government as the only stable one in existence in the republic, and a political meeting in New York displaying such banners as "Enlarge the Bounds of Liberty," and "No British Interference on the American Continent," and Buchanan, nominated as candidate of the Democratic party in place of Pierce standing also for Walker by the declaration that, "in view of so commanding an interest, the people of the United States cannot but sympathize with the efforts being made by the people of Central America to regenerate that portion of the continent which covers the passage across the interoceanic isthmus."

One asks what were Walker's purposes in Central America, and takes the judgment of the historian and biographer on whom all later writers depend for much of their information, William Scroggs.

> Briefly, [he says] he planned to create out of five Central American republics a strong federated State organized and governed on military principles; and after achieving this he aimed to effect the conquest of Cuba. To aid in the work of conquest and in the subsequent "regeneration" of the isthmus and island, he purposed to introduce an American population and to secure to it the possession of the land. . . . Finally, as the capstone of his system, he planned to make the dream of an interoceanic canal come true. . . . It should be added that over this tropical federation, Walker himself proposed to play the role of dictator.

As Walker's power increased, with new recruits arriving on every ship, the other Central American States became alarmed and were ready, with Costa Rica leading, and Vanderbilt taking an active part in supplying funds and arms, to take an active part against the North Americans. They invaded Nicaragua, took León, and drove Walker and his forces back to Granada, which he finally lost. His ships were defeated in battle, and his forces finally starved into surrender by the action of Vanderbilt in withdrawing his boats and of the great powers in sending their fleets to prevent the movement of ships.

Through this confusion of international politics President Mora moved, sending his army when needed, appealing to European powers for protection, issuing with a new Nicaraguan President a manifesto against the United States and then withdrawing it with an apology for the misunderstanding which had caused it. On May 1, 1857, Walker surrendered, not to the Central Americans but to the commander of a United States warship, who had arranged safe conduct to the United States for him and such of his men as desired. He was to make another attempt in 1860 and be shot in Honduras. But with his departure in 1857, the native resistance to filibustering could end. Vanderbilt never revived his Transit Company. Transcontinental railways in the United States drew the stream of travel which had, for those few years, flowed across the Isthmus. Mora's work as the leader of the native resistance was done, and the United States was plunged into Civil War. By the time this conflict was over, the whole North American picture had changed, and the Central American one was also in process of change.

THE END OF THE CHAPTER

Costa Ricans would be glad if they could remember the defender of their country as closing his days peacefully. But politics in the disturbed republic forced Mora to leave the country, after he had been elected in 1859 to the presidency for a third time. Driven out by a revolution, he came to the United States, but returned in 1860 to lead a counter revolution. He was given protection in the British consulate and might have escaped, but word came to him that if he gave himself up, the lives of his brothers and several of his friends would be spared. He was shot in the same month of September that saw William Walker meet a like fate in Honduras.

Costa Ricans remember Juan Rafael Mora for his deeds of peace as well as those of war. In the years of his first presidency, he did much for the republic. He furthered the coffee industry, which was to become Costa Rica's principal source of wealth. He favored education, founding schools of medicine and law and making attendance at primary schools compulsory for children. He built many public buildings, among them the first National Museum and a theater, and he established the first national bank. The works of peace belonged to the pleasant, popular, capable merchant. The works of war did not. His opponents complained of the cruelty of his treatment of those whom his armies defeated. He was thrust into an international quarrel which was beyond his powers to meet. But we of the United States are not the ones to condemn him when he was following the natural impulse to defend his country against unwarranted aggression by citizens of our own country, of whom he believed the worst that could be said. Central Americans may well honor him for his determined stand on behalf of their independence.

ZAMORA OF COSTA RICA

ZAMORA OF COSTA RICA

"Costa Rica prides itself on having more school-teachers than soldiers."—Samuel Crowther, in 1929.

WHILE its neighbor Guatemala remembers with pride its pioneer educator-President of the early days of independence, Mariano Galvez, Costa Ricans honor the founder of their compulsory school system, a man who took the presidency of the little, progressive republic in the period of our Civil War. The name of the dictator Tomás Guardia, who succeeded him, is far better known. Guardia worked with Minor Keith to give the country railroads and did much to break up the system of government by a few aristocratic families which owned large portions of the land. He ruled for a dozen years, now in one office and now in another, and made himself known outside the country as well as at home. But the quiet, able man who came before him in the presidency had laid the foundation on which he tried to build a new social order.

PHYSICIAN AND GOVERNOR

This man whose name sounds truly Spanish to our northern ears was Jesus Jimenez Zamora, born in 1823 in the city of Cartago into one of the leading families of the country. Like other lads who proved their brilliance in the lower schools, he went to Guatemala City for his higher education, studying at the University there and coming home after his long student period there with degrees which gave him the right to practice as physician and surgeon. But he was not to be allowed to continue long in the profession where he proved himself even as a young man to have exceptional ability.

Cartago is the ancient capital of Costa Rica, founded in 1564. In spite of the name "rich coast," given by the sixteenth century explorers, Costa Rica lacked the gold and silver which were demanded in those days. Lying south of Nicaragua and far from Guatemala City, which was the seat of government of the Spanish Captaincy-General, it attracted little attention down the centuries, being regarded as a weak little colony so inaccessible as to make it of small importance to the empire. The interior of the country was thickly wooded and hard to penetrate, though the Franciscan friars found their way there and did a beautiful work. There is the pleasant picture of one of these first missionaries, Fray Betanzos, who learned the many Indian dialects and traveled up and down the country, barefoot according to the European rule of his Order and accompanied only by a small boy who assisted him in his services. The Spanish historian Vasquez pays this tribute to the gentle and energetic friar: "During the sixteen years while he thus labored, there was not a palm of territory in the province which he did not cover in his search for souls."

From those early days dated Cartago, on the beautiful highlands of the interior, not far from the Pacific coast but separated by the chain of high mountains which form the backbone of the entire Isthmus from the unexplored lands that sloped down to the Caribbean Sea. Cartago was no longer the capital in the days when Jimenez was growing up in it, for with the movement for independence had gone the moving of the seat of government to the nearby city of San José. It was a lovely old Spanish town in the center of a farming district which had been increasingly given to coffee culture as the century went on. Zamora became its Governor and came to know the district thoroughly during the days of holding that office.

In 1850 he married Doña Esmeralda Oreamuno, daughter of another of the chief families of the country, and to that home came seven children, one of whom Ricardo, known as Don Ricardo Jimenez Oreamuno, after the custom of carrying on the mother's name, became President of Costa Rica in 1910 and 1924. There was a presidency in the family on the mother's side, too, when an ancestor held office back in 1844. Don Jimenez and his delightful wife represented the best of the Conservative aristocracy.

AS PRESIDENT

First in the Chamber of Deputies of Costa Rica, and then in the Cabinet of President Montealegre, he gained

—: 197 :—

experience and made himself known by his progressive views. Under President Mora Costa Rica was drawn into the war with the American filibusters, led by William Walker, sending armies to expel them from Nicaragua. In that period the cholera epidemic took a toll of ten to twelve thousand persons and paralyzed the life of the country. But by 1863 the country had returned to its normal condition.

Zamora came to the headship of the State with more than usual approval by the people of both parties, and took advantage of his office to build schools and highways and in all ways to promote education. It was, however, in a later term as Provisional President, in 1869, after he had been thrown out of office by political strife and then returned, that he was able to do the thing by which he is chiefly remembered. He wrote into the constitution of Costa Rica that primary education should be required for all children, and that it should be at the expense of the nation.

Public education with public funds was a great step forward for a Central American republic in those times. Only in Costa Rica could it have been accomplished by such a decree. It paved the way for the present highly respected educational system of the republic. Democracy has had its chance for success in a country where the land is farmed in small estates by men who own it and work it, and three generations have gone to public school as a natural and normal part of citizenship.

TWO MODERN SCHOOL BUILDINGS
Costa Rica has created a democracy by special attention
to public education.

BENITO JUAREZ, MEXICO'S INDIAN HERO

BENITO JUAREZ, MEXICO'S INDIAN HERO

"He not only laid the foundations of constitutional liberty, education, and commercial development, but saved his country from the imperial rule of a foreign power.— I. S. Bartlett, United States Collector of Customs, 1865.

FROM the turmoil of Central American affairs in the middle of the nineteenth century, the story of Benito Juarez brings us back to a village some four hundred miles west of the border of the present Guatemalan republic, northwest of the Gulf of Tehuantepec. The life of this man whom Mexico has chosen for its representative in the Gallery of Patriots in Washington was to be lived in the midst of national disturbances, but its serene beginnings may have contributed to the calm which he maintained in his dealings with friends and opponents alike.

A PROUD INHERITANCE

It was a little mountain village, beyond the town of Ixtlan, now known as Ixtlan de Juarez, where the boy was born, on March 21, 1806, to Marcelino Juarez and Brigida Garcia, both pure-blooded Indians, and given in the church the name of Benito Pablo. Here in Oaxaca had

dwelt for almost all the years since the beginning of the
Christian era the Toltecs, an advanced race which conquered the Mayans and then lived with them, absorbing
many of their ideas and ways. The great hero of the
Toltecs was the wise ruler Quetzalcoatl, whose name and
fame is known to all students of the ancient American
peoples who inhabited this region before the coming of
the white men. In the days of their power, when they
were ruling the land from Mexico City to Yucatan, these
Toltecs built massive cities, surpassing those of the Mayas.
A two-hundred-foot-high pyramid for the worship of the
Sun God is thought to be the tallest structure erected any-
where in North America by the aboriginals.

Of such a race came the Juarez family, and of a tribe
within that race, the Zapotecs, who occupied southwestern
Mexico and surpassed their neighbors in architectural
skill. The ruins of their sacred city, Mitla, which was not
more than fifty miles from Benito's home, had been re-
discovered and brought to the attention of archaeologists
from Europe and the United States in the years when the
boy was growing up. The Central American delegate to
Iturbide's Congress, Valle, had visited them on his home-
ward journey from Mexico City. Mr. Stephens had been
attracted to the Isthmus by the reports of these and other
newly found ruins, and other travelers of the time report
on them. "The monuments of the golden age of Greece
and of Rome," said a French archaeologist, "alone equal
the beauty of the Zapotec Palace at Mitla." The ruins of a

A ZAPOTECAN WOMAN OF TODAY
So might have looked the mother or the grandmother
of Benito Juarez.

city, laid out around open courts and built on low terraces, with mosaic stone sculpture covering both outer and inner walls of the buildings, remained as evidence of the high culture of this people.

Even more interesting is the conclusion of scholars that the Toltecs excelled in government, and handed on to the Aztecs, whose empire succeeded their own, a rich inheritance along this as well as architectural lines. A pureblooded Zapotec Indian, like Benito Juarez, had every right to develop the instinct for government which brought him to the highest office in the Mexican republic.

HIS LIFE IN OAXACA

Benito's father and mother were Indian peasants, cultivating their own small piece of land, with its well-tilled fields and small orchard, and he lived that same simple life after he was left an orphan at the age of three to be brought up by his grandmother and his uncle. At the age of twelve he had had no schooling, and did not know how to read or write. Nor did he speak Spanish, the ruling language of the empire beyond the valley where Hidalgo and Morelos were waging their fight for independence and for greater opportunity for the native peoples. But he had acquired a habit of hard work and a training in the simple honesty and sturdy independence of a mountain race which lived its life with little attention to the great world outside.

There was a spark of independence, too, which made Benito leave his village and go down at the age of twelve to the capital of the province, the city of Oaxaca, thirty miles away. Here he was taken into the home of a book-binder, Antonio Salanueva, who was one of the lesser clergy, having become a member of the Third Order of St. Francis. This educated Franciscan took a great inter-est in the boy who had come to his household to serve him, and taught him not only the Spanish language but also the elementary studies of the schools. When his pupil showed uncommon intelligence, he encouraged him to go further, with a view to entering the Church. Even in those days a few promising Indians were allowed to train for minor offices in the priesthood, and young Juarez entered at fifteen the ecclesiastical seminary at Oaxaca, attending as a day student while he continued to live in the home of Fray Antonio, and absorbing with eagerness the studies there taught.

The year 1824 saw the beginning of a new day in Mex-ico. The would-be emperor, Iturbide, had been deposed in the previous year, and now a new constitution was adopted, patterned somewhat on that of the United States, with the country broken up into States, of which the province of Oaxaca was one, and the control of the gov-ernment to be in the hands of a president, a vice-president, a house of deputies, and a senate. The first head of the Republic was Guadalupe Victoria, a well-meaning and popular Mexican, who stood for progressive measures. A

strong movement for education followed, in which
Oaxaca shared by the founding in 1826 of a local Institute
of Arts and Sciences. Juarez left the Church seminary to
continue his studies in this new school, where he remained
for two years. At the age of twenty-three he was given the
honor of appointment to the professorship of Experimental Physics in the Government College. Here he
taught and studied until he obtained the degree of Bachelor of Law in 1832, being admitted as an advocate of the
Supreme Court of the Republic in 1834.

In his valuable biography of Juarez the British student
of Mexican affairs, Mr. U. R. Burke, sums up the next
few years.

> No thoughtful man in Mexico at that time could fail
> to take the keenest interest in political affairs; no honest
> man could fail to assist, to the utmost of his capacity, in
> the peaceful development of his country.

> In the early part of 1831, Juarez accepted the modest
> but onerous post of *Regidor del ayuntamiento,* of Judicial
> Secretary to the Municipal Council of Oaxaca. In the next
> year he was elected by his native State to be their Deputy
> to the National Congress at Mexico, which met in August,
> 1832. The Congress was dissolved in December, when
> Santa Anna, after a brief campaign, once more made him-
> self absolute ruler of the country. And Juarez, who hated
> intrigue and bloodshed, and loved hard work and peace-
> ful study, both legal and scientific, withdrew himself
> cheerfully from the arena of political strife, and led, for
> the next ten years, the simple and uneventful life of a
> provincial lawyer.

That peace which the biographer describes was broken by a brief term in prison. He had protested against the series of acts by which Santa Anna, as represented by one of his lieutenants, swept aside the State and other local governments which were not yielding to his absolute authority, called for a new Congress, and finally for a new constitution that deprived the States of their independence. The young Indian lawyer was soon released, and the chief other event of this period was his marriage in 1843 to Doña Margarita Maza, a beautiful lady of Spanish background who from that time supported him in his public as well as his private life.

AS GOVERNOR OF OAXACA

In the national life of Mexico the record of Juarez in these years is one of steady opposition to Santa Anna whenever that dictator was in power and of brief returns to Mexico City to represent his State when there was an interval of popular, liberal rule. Such a time came in 1846 when a Constituent Assembly was summoned, and he stayed on to vote as he pleased in spite of the fact that Santa Anna unexpectedly returned. These were the years of the annexation of Texas by the United States and of the war between the two countries by which Mexico lost other territory. It seems remarkable that Juarez could go back to Oaxaca, where he had been elected Governor in 1847, and have five years of peaceful administration of that southern State.

The only way to measure the achievements of this quiet, capable Indian leader is by comparing them with those of men of other provinces. He found the public treasury empty, the troops unruly from a long period without pay and because of the disorganized condition of the country, and the administration of justice by the courts practically worthless. His first step was to reëstablish his own college, the Institute of Arts and Sciences which Santa Anna, in his impatience at all popular education, had disbanded. Juarez also built roads to connect the different parts of the State. He restored the courts, won the soldiers back to proper discipline, and began to pay off the State debt by the prompt collection of taxes. His legal training enabled him to draw up a code of laws which was copied in other States. In many respects the State came to be a model to which others turned in their problems, and the name of the Governor was known far beyond its limits. Calm, honest, quiet efficiency was too little known in public office not to attract attention and comment. Especially was it noted that he ruled without violence. "The shootings and imprisonments, the confiscations and banishments, of former days, were absolutely unknown," comments one who is writing about these days.

In 1853, however, Santa Anna returned from exile in South America and restored the old, autocratic rule, with himself in the supreme place as dictator, with the title of "Most Serene Highness," and clergy and landowners who held vast estates supporting him. One of his first acts was to order the arrest of Governor Juarez, who had incurred his displeasure by his courageous opposition in the Assembly and also by a refusal to allow him to enter the State of Oaxaca when he was a fugitive from Mexico City.

IN EXILE AND BACK

Juarez was arrested on May 30, 1853, without even the form of an accusation or the show of a trial, and was sent to the castle of San Juan de Ulloa, a fortress in the harbor of Veracruz. There he was thrown into a vile dungeon below the level of the sea, where he was to be held indefinitely. By great good fortune he managed to escape by the end of that summer, and boarded an English ship which landed him in Havana.

From that port he made his way to New Orleans, where he arrived almost penniless. For nearly two years he lived there, a stranger in a strange land, with hardly money enough to buy food to keep from starving. In such a case other exiles from the countries to the south busied themselves with intrigues for return to power. The Indian went calmly about making the study which he had long desired to undertake of the English language and of constitutional law.

There in New Orleans good news came to him of a new gathering of the forces for liberalism in Mexico and of the making of a new "plan" or platform of principles, the Plan of Ayutla, so named from the town where it was

BENITO PABLO JUAREZ
1806 - 1872

made. Juarez returned to Mexico, took part in the struggle
to oust Santa Anna and his forces, and was made Minister
of Justice and Religion in the Cabinet of the new President, Juan Alvarez, another full-blooded Indian from the
south who had led in the revolt.

Here he devised the new law, which was shortly
adopted, by which old ecclesiastical courts were robbed of
their special privileges, and all priests and soldiers were
brought under the authority of the civil courts. This important reform measure, which set up impartial justice for
all, was known as the *Ley Juarez,* the Juarez Law. The
reaction against this bold act sent him into retirement, as
the leaders shifted in his political party, and he spent a
year as Governor again of Oaxaca. But he was in constant touch with the men in the Assembly who were working for reform, and other laws aimed at the breaking up
of the huge landownings of the Church were benefited in
their wording by his legal knowledge. There were many
able men working toward the same ends, but there seems
to have been a quality in this strong, clear headed, honest
man which made his word important in the counsels of
his party.

A WANDERING PRESIDENT

In 1857 the new constitution in the making of which he
had had a large share was put into effect by the decree of
the President. Into it was written a bold program, too
bold and progressive, apparently, for the time. Here were

provisions for freedom of the press, freedom of assembly, equal civil rights for all men, complete religious toleration, and the abolition of all the long-time special privileges and monopolies which had stood in the way of progress. These men were following in the steps of Hidalgo and Morelos, but now as in those earlier days the effort to deprive the rich landowners and the Church officials of their almost unbounded power roused tremendous forces of opposition.

Conditions were so critical that Governor Juarez yielded to the urgency of the constitution's supporters and came to Mexico City in advance of its adoption to lend his influence for it. Before the new document had been in force a month, there was threat of revolution, and the Ministry resigned. In another month Juarez had been appointed Chief Justice of the Supreme Court and Vice-President of the United States of Mexico. By the beginning of the year 1858 the President had fled to the safe shelter of the United States, and Juarez became constitutional President in his place. Meanwhile the opposition, backed by the army and the Church, had chosen another President, and one of the first moves of President Juarez was to announce that he would defend the constitution by force, if need be.

He and his government were soon forced out of Mexico City, and his first, hastily gathered army met a defeat. He and his Cabinet retired to Guadalajara, three hundred miles from the capital, and from this spot comes an extraordinary tale of treachery and bravery. The colonel in command of the little garrison there, a soldier who had protested his loyalty, saw in Juarez' presence a chance to assert his power. He and his men took their captive guests prisoners and kept them under guard in one room while they, in the next room, made their terms. They offered President Juarez his liberty if he would send orders back to his supporters to abandon the city to the opposition, and when this proposal was rejected, the Colonel sent a line of soldiers into the room where the officials waited, and told them to shoot the prisoners.

Juarez had happened to go to the far end of the room. As the soldiers formed in line, he came forward and stood opposite to them, his black eyes turned on the muskets which were levelled at him and his companions. As he gazed at them, the word was given to fire. But the soldiers hesitated under his gaze, and then grounded their arms.

THE WAR OF REFORM

A loyal force shortly came to his rescue, but he knew that he must move on, and he desired to reach the loyal city of Veracruz. He could not safely cross the republic, but had to go to the nearby Pacific coast, embark on an American vessel for Panama, cross the Isthmus and go north by ship to New Orleans, and thence to Veracruz, where he arrived some seven weeks later. From that time the seat of the government was "wherever Juarez happened to be," as the Mexican historian, Teja Zabre, puts it, adding that he was followed by the "greatest, most sincere, and most loyal men of his party." Defeat and poverty, he continues, also followed them. "Fugitives and wanderers, the reformist leaders were on the point of falling for all time." The four-year civil war which followed was, according to this historian, the "cruellest and longest civil war in the history of Mexico"; and a reading of the list of its engagements inclines one to agree with him.

The reform movement of President Juarez, was, however, united under the one leader, and maintained through the years its seat of government in Veracruz, where in 1859 it was officially recognized by the United States. That was a great step forward for Juarez, but it was somewhat counterbalanced by the fact that the European nations were recognizing the changing government at Mexico City, which had at least two contending leaders. This European situation, which was to lead to armed intervention, was aggravated by the loss of large amounts of money, stolen from the British Legation or in transit across the country by those contending for the power and holding their own against Juarez.

However, the tide gradually turned in his favor, and in January of 1861 he was able to enter Mexico City in triumph, restored to the capital over which he had been, by the constitution and election of 1857, the lawful President for all these years. At Veracruz he had issued decrees continuing his program of reform. Now he was able to make these acts effective. By this means, says Rogelio Alfaro, he "sought to end the feudalistic state in which the clergy and landed aristocracy had kept the country." The war just ended became known as the "War of Reform," as the earlier struggles of Hidalgo and Morelos had been in a "War for Independence." If Mexico could now have been left alone to arrange its own affairs in such peace as the reformers might attain, happier days might soon have come.

INTERVENTION FROM ABROAD

There is disagreement over the skill of this lawyer-ruler in the trying task of reconstruction with which he was confronted. With no foreign intervention, it would have been a desperate task, and Benito Juarez, for all his honesty and calm strength of purpose, had had no preparation for such an office.

The chaos and anarchy of the previous years had brought the European nations to the point of taking over the control of Mexico's affairs in an effort to get their debts paid and their losses restored. When the Congress deferred payment on all debts because of the bankruptcy of the government, the storm broke. France, Spain, and England agreed to occupy ports of Mexico and collect customs for the payment of their debts. In 1862 armies of these three nations were landed in Mexico, and while the troops of the other two soon withdrew the French stayed. Napoleon III had designs on Mexico. He was then at the height of his power, and had doubtless been assured by

Mexican exiles, defeated by the Reform government, that there were many in the country who would welcome a monarch such as he might choose to send them from Europe.

In 1862 French troops were marching on Mexico, and President Juarez was calling on his fellow-citizens to defend their country from invasion. The day which Mexicans remember with pride is that of May 5, 1862, when gallant resistance was put up by their soldiers at Puebla and a French army of greater size than that of the defenders was repulsed. *El Cinco de Mayo* is one of the national holidays, and General Zaragoza is remembered with honor because of his brilliant victory. But more and more French troops were sent to the field.

At the end of that May Juarez was forced to abandon the capital. Again he became a wandering President, with his forces driven slowly back in spite of heroic efforts. By the end of 1863 he had been compelled to move farther and farther north till he came to the frontier town of El Paso del Norte (now known as Ciudad Juarez), within sight of the United States territory and across the border from El Paso, Texas. There is preserved in the National Museum the black carriage of the President, which carried him farther and farther north to this spot, while the French troops were advancing and the Archduke Maximilian and his wife Carlota were landing in Veracruz and proceeding across the country to Mexico City. There Maximilian was received as emperor, and one of the strangest chapters in the history of the American hemisphere began.

The Emperor might seem to be ruling with all pomp and splendor in the national capital, but waiting on the border was Benito Juarez, who extended his term as President beyond November of 1864 in the national emergency. The tall, fair-haired Austrian prince, with his blond beard and his gentle, friendly manner, might issue his decrees and hope that he was indeed, as the conservatives at first declared, the choice of the people. But the quiet, dark-haired, black-eyed Indian head of the State was waiting in the north, and no number of French troops such as could be sent could occupy or control the great expanse of Mexican territory that stretched as far as Central America to the south.

ON THE BORDER OF TEXAS

It is our good fortune that an American journalist, Mr. I. S. Bartlett, was in El Paso at the time of the arrival of President Juarez, and came to know him well during the ten months when he conducted his government in the Mexican town across the border. He describes him as he appeared on the day when, with other American officials, he went to call on him in the attractive adobe house where he was living.

I saw before me a descendant of the Aztec Zapotec race, of pure lineage, a short, solidly built, thick-set man, a little over five feet high, with a face darkly bronzed, handsome dark eyes, high cheek bones, a strong prominent nose, and black hair cut short. His expression of countenance was winning. His manner was that of a cultivated gentleman and scholar, easy and dignified. His conversation lacked the fluency and vehemence characteristic of the Spanish. His voice was low and pleasant, and he frequently paused as if weighing the import of his words. His dress was that of a citizen President, and, from an American point of view, faultless. He wore coat and trousers of black broadcloth, a white linen vest, standing collar, black necktie, white kid gloves, and highly polished boots. His hair was cut short and his face was smoothly shaven.

Mr. Bartlett was at this time acting United States collector of customs, and attended the famous ball which was tendered to President Juarez on November 10, 1865, when the French forces were retreating and he was preparing to return to a place nearer his capital. The President was touched by the expression of friendship, but when the suggestion was made that the reception be in El Paso, he said quietly that he could never accept any invitation which would take him outside of Mexico.

"I have resolved," he continued, "never to leave the soil of Mexico during its occupation by foreign invaders."

The reception was therefore held in the Mexican city. An American lady who attended it remarked that "No one could have imagined, as they saw him laughing and chatting gaily away, that he had on his shoulders all the cares of a tottering government and of an empty treasury."

THE REPUBLIC AGAIN

American concern over the French occupation of Mexico had been strong from the first, but our people were in the midst of their own Civil War. It was doubtless this conflict, with the idea held by Napoleon III that the Confederate States might well be victorious and separate from the North for the formation of a southern empire, which had encouraged the European nations to ignore the Monroe Doctrine, with its strong words against such occupation. With the close of that war many Union soldiers went to the support of Juarez, and on December 16, 1865, Secretary Seward issued a protest to the French government against the continued presence of their troops in Mexico. Napoleon III began to withdraw his army, and Emperor Maximilian had to decide whether to go with them or remain. In the end he remained, hoping for more support, and was forced to yield to the advancing forces of Juarez. In May of 1867 he surrendered and in June was shot. That fall Juarez was again elected President of Mexico. Again he had to try to establish a strong rule and reconcile warring elements of the parties. He was crushing such a revolt when on July 18, 1872, he died at the age of sixty-six years.

Of him Teja Zabre says: "Just as Hidalgo and Morelos, being the first and greatest, represented the liberating movement of 1810 . . . ; just as Iturbide stands for the transition between the colonial period and that of independence; just as Santa Anna is the outstanding figure of the alternating periods of military dictatorship and anarchy that went on until the middle of the nineteenth century, so Juarez is Mexico's representative personality during the period of Reform, the Intervention, and the Empire."

Secretary Seward, who visited him in Mexico after the Civil War, said in a speech at Puebla, "Juarez is the greatest man I ever met in my life."

One of his biographers says that the work of his life was the setting of Law above Force in Mexico.

BARRIOS, THE REFORMER

BARRIOS, THE REFORMER

*"If we have to wait to accomplish any-
thing until there are no difficulties in the
way, nothing will ever get done."*—Barrios.

"A DICTATOR," the historian Wilgus has remarked, "is a 'do-it-now' man in a land of
mañana [tomorrow]." He could not have better described the man whom Guatemala has named as its leading patriot of the nineteenth century, Justo Rufino Barrios, whose birthday is celebrated each year as a national
holiday. From the time he was a small boy, Rufino Barrios did things now, instead of waiting till tomorrow.
The result was that he pushed his nation out of the past
and into the modern world in a dozen years, accomplishing what would normally have taken a full generation or
more. But the method of his doing it was that of the well-
meaning but ruthless dictator. He knew this himself and
justified it, declaring that his method was necessary. "My
mission," he said, in one of his documents signed as President of the Republic, "has been that of a dictator whose
role did not permit him to give liberty, but only to prepare for it." The preparation included schools, hospitals,
railways, highways, telegraphs, and a series of laws issued

so fast that his Congress could not keep up with him in ratifying them.

A LIVELY BOY

As a small boy of ten, he had the idea that it would be fun to make a burro ride on the back of a mule. So, with the help of one of his father's servants, he managed to get the smaller animal up on the back of the larger. But the burro struggled, the mule kicked and plunged and backed, and the neck of the burro was broken. If that had been the first mischief he had done, it might have been over-looked. But it was the climax of a series of escapades in which he had led the boys of his native village of San Lorenzo in southwestern Guatemala, near the border of Mexico. His father decided that stern measures were nec-essary, and put him to serve with the muleteers, who traveled back and forth from the coast lands of the Pacific up into the mountains of the Sierra Madre, where the vil-lage of San Lorenzo was located.

That was a hard life for a boy who was son of one of the wealthiest men of the region. José Ignacio Barrios had been a dealer in horses and cattle before he married Joséfa Anyon, daughter of the wealthy Anyon family which owned thousands of acres in the highlands and on the coast, and since his marriage he had done well in busi-ness. Justo Rufino, born July 19, 1835, was the fourth in a family of seven children, who lived in a long adobe house roofed with thatch, alongside of the houses of others of the Anyon family. That house is shown today to those who come on pilgrimage up into the mountains to see the birthplace of the patriot, and the tale is told of how the young couple, when they set up housekeeping, planted a cherry tree and a peach tree in their yard and three eucalyptus trees just outside, with a hedge to shut their courtyard in. San Lorenzo was only a little village on a lower ridge of Tacumulco, Central America's highest volcano, which had been for a long time calm and silent. But it was a *ladino* village, not a wholly Indian settlement, the name *ladino* being used for Spanish-speaking white or *mestizo* people. Here were mountaineers who got their living by cultivating the barren soil or by tending cattle on the ranches, hard-working, independent men who lived their own lives and thought their own thoughts, regardless of the city folk on the lowlands.

The village life was not easy, but it must have seemed so to young Rufino when he went with the muleteers, being set at first to ride the single mare which always led a mule train. These men carried down from the hills the articles which had been made there, flour ground in their mills, cloth woven on the looms, pottery made at the kilns, and exchanged these loads on the coast for the products of the land, coffee, sugar, fruits that grew in the tropic heat, and such articles as came from overseas. On each trip they went from the cold of the heights into the heat of the tropics, sleeping always in the open air whether it was the rainy season or the dry. Rufino bore the hardships well, and did his part in the managing of the stubborn beasts and the heavy loading and unloading. He grew taller and stronger in those years, and learned to take orders from those above him and to hold his own with the other boys and men.

AT SCHOOL AND COLLEGE

Then, when he was fourteen, some one mocked him because he could not read. That taunt sank deep, and Rufino resolved that such a thing should never be said to him again. With the speed of action that was to be his mark all through his life, he went home and presented himself to the sacristan, who lived in the church buildings at San Lorenzo, where there was no priest, and was the school teacher for the village.

"I want to learn to read," he told the man, and was set at once to learn the long catechism, a task which occupied a whole winter in the schoolroom, but which Rufino put through in a brief two or three weeks.

His parents were pleased at his desire to learn and sent him over the mountain road the twelve miles to the town of San Marcos, where he could study further. From there he went to the Jesuit College in the city of Quezaltenango, the center for all that region. There he learned Latin and the other studies belonging to the regular course, and a year later went on to the famous *Escuela de Cristo,* in the capital of the republic, fifty miles or so farther east. There he did well in his studies, and became known, as he had

JUSTO RUFINO BARRIOS
1835 - 1885

in his village, as a leader, ready for any escapade. Guatemala City was a typical Spanish-American city, with its aristocratic youth at the University leading a gay, fashionable life, with much card playing and betting on horses and cock fighting. Rufino Barrios took his part in the student life, but he was made to know the social difference between himself, as a son of a ranch owner coming from a little mountain village, and the young aristocrats of the cities. There is a story of his having loaned a book to a fellow student, and, when it was not returned, going to the wealthy home of the young man to ask for it. It was raining heavily that day, and the servant who came to the door did not ask young Barrios in, but left him standing in the rain while he went in search of the son of the house. When the student came, he brought the book and explained, excusing himself, that he had not come to return it as he "might catch cold if he came out in the rain on such a day."

"But common folk like me have to stand out in the rain even if it kills them," answered Barrios bitterly, and went away to meditate gloomily on the differences between social classes. Years later when he was President of the Republic, he delighted in shocking the aristocrats by some rough jest or prank, remembering, doubtless, these days when he felt himself humiliated.

These were the days when Carrera, the Indian revolutionist, was at the height of his power as "Life-President of Guatemala," exercising absolute authority and ruling with harshness and brutality. As a student Barrios heard much political talk, and knew of the measures by which Carrera kept himself in power, the torturing of his victims, the constant fighting with his enemies, and the wholesale executions of those who fell under his displeasure. The wiser citizens of the country were cautioning patience and biding their time, but there was constant information of the efforts of neighbor republics along the lines of free government and constant discussion among the students. During Barrios' student days came the "Filibuster War", when the republics united to expel William Walker and his army from Nicaragua. Ten men came down from the village of San Lorenzo, in accordance with Carrera's levy for troops, and young Barrios went to their camp in Guatemala City to visit with them while they were in training and gave to each five dollars. To them he was like the young squire in an English village, the son of one of their leading families.

ON HIS RANCH

His student days ended, with a degree of Bachelor of Philosophy, and a knowledge of law which had enabled him to pass the examination and become a Notary Public, Rufino Barrios returned to San Marcos in 1862 and opened a law office. His father gave him at this time a present of a plantation just over the border in Mexican territory, known as "The Malacate." The combination of office and plantation just suited Barrios' restless spirit. He could experiment in crops and in stock raising, try out new breeds of cattle to improve his stock, and amuse himself with horses, games of chance in the nearby towns, and the sport of cock fighting. Coffee was just beginning to be grown in Guatemala in his student days, and he began now to grow it on his land, being the first to pioneer with it on the west coast. He tried out cotton, too, but could not do much with it because there were no mills, and the transportation over the mountains or by water was too expensive to make its growing profitable. But under and through all his activities as planter and notary ran a restlessness of mind that led him into new ideas of government and lines of liberal thought. He was becoming a revolutionist in thought, if not yet in deed, and his plantation, being over the line in Mexico, was an excellent spot for safe discussion of revolutionary ideas.

A DARING FIGHTER

After Carrera died in 1865, more and more of the dissatisfied young men of the western country found their way to "The Malacate" to plan and plot, and in 1867 Barrios with other military leaders, crossed the border, took San Marcos and other nearby towns, and created such a disturbance that government troops were sent to clear them out. Barrios was wounded and imprisoned, but escaped to Mexico, whither had fled other leaders, notably Miguel Garcia Granados, an older man, deputy of the Guatemalan Congress, who had been expelled by Carrera's successor and was now considered the leader of the opposition. He was a man of wealth, experience in politics, and prestige in Guatemala City, who was to equip and lead the "Army of Liberation," which was to free Guatemala from the regime which had held it back under oppressive tyranny for so long. Barrios, young, personally attractive, popular, a daring fighter, was to be his able lieutenant. When the two entered Guatemala, the "army" consisted of fourteen officers and fourteen soldiers! But recruits flocked to their standard. The west country was eager for a new government, and Granados was skilful in issuing eloquent proclamations which called the people to replace the old, outworn regime with a popular and progressive government, under which all classes should receive justice. Barrios did his part as general in the fighting, and after a three months' campaign the "Army of Liberation" entered the capital as victors, on June 30, 1871. It is to their credit that they took possession without looting or disorder. When Guatemala celebrates, as it does each year, the thirtieth of June as the day of triumph of the liberal revolution, it is remembered that when Granados and his generals appeared on the balcony of the government building, and the cry went up from the people, "Death to the conquered," the reply of Granados was: "No, no, be still. We desire death for no one. Liberty does not need blood in order to flourish. This is too grand and glorious a day to stain with such cries."

Dr. Ramon Salazar, who saw Barrios enter the city with

Courtesy of Guatemalan Legation, Washington, D. C.

NATIONAL INSTITUTE AND MEDICAL SCHOOL, GUATEMALA CITY
University education in Guatemala has a long and
distinguished history.

the "Army of Liberation," describes him as he appeared at this time. He was thirty-five years of age, of medium height and robust appearance. His hands were small; his mouth broad, but his lips not thick. "He had a wide forehead," he continues, "and when he was calm, no wrinkle was to be seen in it. But if anything angered him, the tempest in his soul was easily visible on his brow. He always wore his hair clipped short. His eye was lively and penetrating. Whether due to a strong magnetic power, or whether it was that everybody was afraid of him, I do not know; but the fact remains that I never saw any person who could withstand his glance."

Portraits of that period show Barrios as the adventurer, the guerilla fighter, wearing the customary broad-brimmed hat of the tropics, and carrying always, instead of a sword, a whip. This whip is mentioned often by those who saw him at this time, and even later, when he was President of the Republic. There is a tale of his walking into a room where were assembled a group of men plotting to assassinate him, and standing there, whip in hand, so cowing them by his look and bold words that they did not lift a hand against him.

AS ACTING PRESIDENT

In the months following the taking over of the government by President Granados, Barrios returned to his plantation, having been given charge of "The West" as his military district. But as clashes came between the reactionary clerical party, which had supported Carrera, and the Liberals, Barrios was repeatedly back in the conflict, taking bold action in expelling the Jesuits from the country, according to Government decree, and putting down armed rebellion in eastern Guatemala and elsewhere. Always in these months, which lengthened into a year and more, Granados was for moderate, harmonizing action, Barrios for immediate measures. At one time when he was Acting President, during Granados's absence on military enterprises, Barrios issued his famous decree for freedom of worship, a document worth quoting as it puts Guatemala in the ranks of the freedom-loving nations of the world.

Signed by "J. Rufino Barrios," March 15, 1872, it reads, in part:

> In view of the fact that one of the most precious liberties of man is that of adoring God according to the dictates of his own conscience, and that liberty of conscience, in order to be real, carries with it the right to worship the Creator according to the belief of each individual, and that this right, won by humanity after centuries of fighting, has been recognized and sanctioned by all the civilized nations of the world. . . . I decree
>
> First, Liberty of Conscience is inviolable in the territory of Guatemala;
>
> Second, the exercise of any and all religions is free in the Republic.

In the decree it is also carefully stated that "freedom of worship is not an attack on the Apostolic Roman Catholic

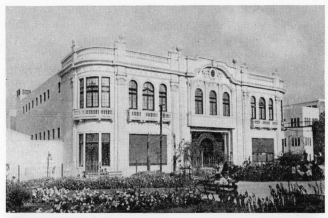

SUPREME COURT BUILDING IN GUATEMALA CITY

Since the opening days of Central American independence, Guatemalan jurists have made important contributions to Latin American Law.

religion, but on the contrary a guarantee for the same, for this religion enjoys all the privileges given any other, as is seen by the fact that liberty of worship exists in the most Catholic countries of the world."

When the last military opposition had been put down on the field of battle, Garcia Granados called for an election for the presidency. He was well along in years, and recognized, doubtless, the popularity of the younger man. Barrios was elected and took office in June, 1873. Now he began to organize the country on his own lines. Of his administration Dr. Adrian Recinos, Minister of Guatemala to Washington in the year 1935, when the centenary of Barrios' birth was being celebrated, gives a thoughtful appraisal.

General Barrios had the gift of surrounding himself with the most competent men of his time and of trusting them to accomplish the most important and lasting part of his work. Through the coöperation of these enlightened men, he bestowed on the country advanced legislation which replaced the heterogeneous collection of ancient Spanish laws—laws of the Indies and of the colonial government. Bringing into the country distinguished teachers from Spain and Spanish America, he modernized public instruction, founded a military school of the first rank, and established normal, vocational and secondary schools for both boys and girls. He multiplied elementary secondary schools throughout the Republic, proclaiming liberty of instruction and making public primary education free, compulsory and lay.

—: 231 :—

HIS GOVERNMENT

It was a government by decree in his first years. He "ordered" one reform after another, from the extension of coffee growing to road building. "I adopted some extraordinary measures," he said to the Assembly in 1876, "some very hard and severe measures against those who disturbed the public order." But he declared that his ruthless acts, the imprisonments, the executions, the taking over of authority were all needed to save the republic in its grave crisis. Always he asserted that dictatorship was in no wise satisfactory to him. "My mission," he declared in one of his final documents, "has been that of a dictator whose role did not permit him to give liberty, but only to prepare for it."

He gave support to the working out of a constitution under which the country should be governed, and was elected under its terms the first constitutional President in 1880. This office he refused for a time, until the Assembly insisted that he accept. Now he was free to do what he could for the material improvement of the country.

As in all the Central American countries mountain barriers and forests and jungles separated the peoples of the different regions. There were the hot lowlands, then the temperate valleys, some four to five thousand feet above sea level, which were the agricultural sections, and then the highlands, above seven thousand feet, where dwelt the mountain people. Barrios saw the need of connecting these regions and set about constructing highways and introducing telegraph lines which should unite the cities and ports and link them with the agricultural sections. He signed a contract for a cable connection with Guatemala, and invited foreign capital to join in the rapid development of the country. The first railway was built, joining the capital, Guatemala City, on its beautiful plateau, five thousand feet above the sea, with its port city of San José. On his forty-ninth birthday, July 19, 1884, while the nation was honoring him by celebration, the first locomotive to arrive in Guatemala was exhibited, with President Barrios in the cab with the engineer, proudly showing the new possession to the admiring populace.

ADVOCATE OF FEDERATION

Two years earlier Barrios had been abroad, coming to Washington to adjust, under arbitration, the boundary between his country and Mexico, going to Europe for a brief tour, and then returning to the United States, where he signed a contract with President Grant for a railroad to connect with the Mexican-Southern road. Back in his home country, after an absence of nearly a half year, he issued an important "order" making the postage rate for any Central American country the same from Guatemala as it was within the national borders.

That was a gesture in the line of his desire for the union of the Central American republics, that dream which had

been written into the constitution of 1879 in a statement
that it was the desire of the republic to join with its sister
nations whenever that became possible. The neighboring
republics had been stimulated to new enterprises by his
energetic example, and he had helped in the support of
liberal governments in El Salvador and Honduras. Now
he began to move toward union. "It is not new to me," he
wrote in a document of February 24, 1883, "to be concerned with the thought of the reconstitution of the Central American Union, sundered in days of unhappy memory. For long I have cherished this idea, because I believe
that it contains the solution of the most interesting problems of our future and that it is the only foundation on
which can be raised the improved structure of these Republics, not only in the material and economic field, but
also in the political and social order."

Again, as was characteristic of him, Barrios could not
wait for the slow development of sentiment for such
union. He and the President of El Salvador proposed to
Honduras, Nicaragua, and Costa Rica the calling of a
Congress which should embody the growing desire for
federation in all the republics and organize some sort of
federated state. When that project failed and it became
evident that Nicaragua and Costa Rica would oppose the
project, Barrios and the Unionists in the various countries decided that an appeal to force was needed. In February of the year 1885 he proclaimed such a union, con-
voking a General Assembly which should draw up the

constitution for a Central American Republic. This meant war by Unionist troops on the countries whose governments opposed the plan.

Guatemala and Honduras stood with Barrios, supplying troops; but by this time the other States had come to feel that he really desired to be dictator of the newly planned State, and even El Salvador, which had stood with him originally, prepared to resist. Still Barrios moved on with his armies, and led personally an attack on the city of Chalchuapa, the fortified stronghold of the Salvadorean troops. In that engagement, in which he insisted on participating himself, he was mortally wounded and died on April 2, 1885.

DICTATOR AND REFORMER

The movement for the Union ended with his death. But the services of the reformer in his own country were written large all over the prosperous land which had come into its own during his twelve years of rule. He had been a dictator, "holding the sword," as some one has said, "constantly over his opponents." But he had stood for the education of the masses and the breaking down of the old aristocratic regime. His excuse for his extreme measures was that only by force could he have accomplished what was needed. Certainly he could not otherwise have accomplished so much in so short a time, and one must always remember that he dealt with a people largely Indian or *mestizo* who had been accustomed always to control by strong leaders. Frankly and disarmingly he wrote his own apologies. "Sometimes," he said in 1880, when he was attempting to resign his office, "I was obliged to cut and burn; and when circumstances demanded it, I conquered my repugnance to cutting and to burning." There are those who criticize him sharply, and those who defend him stoutly. But, looking back on his brief twelve years of rule and the measures which brought Guatemala into line and into relation with the modern world, the people of the republic honor him as a man who helped to liberate them from their past and set them on the road toward the future. They are proud of a native son who could not read at the age of fourteen, but put himself through years of study by his own determination, and came to high office in the service of his country.

"MISTA KEE" — MINOR C. KEITH

"MISTA KEE" — MINOR C. KEITH

"The Costa Ricans dislike wasting their resources in wars or war materials, preferring the arts of peace and to welcome those bringing wealth from other countries."—Laferriere, 1870.

ALONG in the late 1870's fifteen hundred negroes, brought to Costa Rica from the island of Jamaica by Minor C. Keith, young American railroad builder, were toiling in a flood-swept, fever-ridden jungle to lay the tracks of the first railroad in Central America. Indians would not work on that project. White men, brought from New Orleans, had died of fever. Keith had brought a shipload of seven hundred to swampy Limon, on the Caribbean coast, where during the first year of the attempt there had been two hundred and fifty inches of rainfall, and most of them could not survive the climate. Fifteen hundred more had come, and they, too, died of fever. Then he brought Jamaican negroes, and they carried on the work.

But the Costa Rican government, which was coöperating with Mr. Keith in building the road, came to a time when its finances were in difficulty. President Tomás Guardia was borrowing the money in London, and the bottom had dropped out of the bond market. The day came when a large payment was to be made to Keith, and there was no money with which to meet the terms of the agreement. Keith used his own money to meet the payroll of the company until his funds were gone, and still there were no funds.

He called the army of workers together and explained to them exactly what had happened. If they wished to go home to Jamaica, he would pay them for the work they had done that week and arrange for their free transportation home. But he hoped that they would be willing to stay and work without pay until he could get the money needed to carry the project on.

No man wished to leave. All would stay loyally on the job, trusting in Mr. Keith's pledge that the money would be paid in full. But the months went by. It was a year of world-wide financial panic. Costa Rica could not get its money. Keith could not arrange for more. Six months passed, and he had not been able to do anything but feed and clothe the negro workers. Again he called them together, explained how things were, and asked if they would still trust his word. He believed the time would not be long now.

To the Jamaicans Keith had come to seem a miracle worker. They marveled at the daring of a man who would try to carry iron rails across a jungle and up a mountain. But most of all they marveled at the man himself, who managed the work and went smilingly and

"MISTA KEE"—MINOR C. KEITH
1848 - 1929

cheerfully among them, never daunted by disasters and seeming to bear a charmed life when many other white men, among them his own two brothers, fell prey to illness.

Keith called for a vote, and every black hand went up. They would stay and work without pay till the money came. There was just one phrase that they repeated over and over. "Mista Kee will do it." That was their creed, their faith. Though the funds did not come for another three months, the work went on without a pause. When they did come, "Mista Kee" justified their faith in him. He paid them their wages in full and gave them a bonus besides.

This first money came from outside sources, not from the Costa Rican government. When its funds came through and it was able to meet its long-overdue obligation, it, too, acted generously, adding an amount to cover the losses Keith had met because of the long time of waiting.

So Minor Cooper Keith takes his place in Costa Rican and Central American annals, not as a foreigner, but as one who became part of the country's life. Other citizens of the United States came and went, but he stayed. He married a Costa Rican lady, Cristina, daughter of José Marcia Castro, one of the early Presidents of the Republic, and shared in the brilliant social life of the country as well as in the business undertakings which brought in foreign capital.

KEITH'S UNCLE, HENRY MEIGGS

Minor Keith, who was born in Brooklyn in 1848, belonged to an adventuring family. His uncle, his mother's brother, was Henry Meiggs, an up-state New York boy who went into the lumber business and had set himself up in Brooklyn when the gold rush of 'Forty-nine came. He sailed a boatload of lumber around Cape Horn, sold it at a large profit in San Francisco, and stayed to supply the fast-growing town with building materials. Before long he had ships going up and down the coast, bringing wood from forests which his men had discovered. He became one of the leading citizens of the new city, and there was the utmost consternation when the citizens, many of whom had been at a grand party at his fine home on the preceding evening, awoke to be met by the news that he had emptied that house between midnight and dawn, boarded one of his own boats with his family and household goods, and sailed south. He had used his political influence to get a city paving job, and then overdrawn his accounts when he got caught financially on other deals. When he departed he owed the city some $800,000. and other creditors lesser sums.

The ship sailed southward to Chile in South America, and there Henry Meiggs began over again. Here, too, there were pioneer enterprises, and he turned his energy and skill toward accomplishing them. A railroad had been started between the port of Valparaiso and the inland capital, Santiago. Three contractors had failed already, sinking money and time and labor and finding themselves unable to finish the task. Meiggs took the contract and finished ahead of the time he had set and within the sum.

This was the beginning of a career of railroad building which took him from Chile to Peru. Where British and French engineers had declared routes impossible, he allowed nothing to stop him. His roads over the Andes are achievements which are still the wonder of all who visit Peru. "Where a llama can go, I can take a railroad," was his word, and he made good the boast. A stream came in his way, and he turned its waters into another channel, so that he could lay his iron rails in its channel. He swung bridges from one dizzy height to another, zigzagged his tracks back and forth through tunnels and up toward the heights until at one point a passenger on a train could see the road at five different levels, and mounted up, up, up always to the skies, reaching a point 15,200 feet above sealevel as he went inland from the coast.

The financing of these roads was begun in Peru and continued in London. When the Peruvian government had sunk all its funds and practically mortgaged itself to Meiggs, and British financiers had refused to pour in more gold, he still went boldly ahead. It was no wonder that the fame of this man spread all over Latin America, and that Tomás Guardia, when he became President of Costa

—: 243 :—

Rica and desired a railroad within the republic's borders and extending from ocean to ocean, wanted Henry Meiggs to build it. He sent a delegation to Peru to urge the American to take the contract, and Meiggs turned the proposition over to his nephew, Henry Meiggs Keith, Minor Keith's older brother, who had been working with him on the railroads over the Andes.

It is to be noted that Henry Meiggs had paid all his California debts, though he never returned to that State. With all his recklessness, there was a loyalty to those obligations of his younger days.

THE COSTA RICAN RAILWAY

When Henry Keith got that contract from his uncle, he promptly sent for his younger brother, Minor, who was at that time in Texas, to come out and help him. There was more money to be made in this proposition than in anything he was doing there.

Minor had had an extraordinary business for a young man hardly twenty-two. He had chosen to leave school at sixteen, going into business instead of to college, and had gone into the lumber business for himself when he was only seventeen. Then his father had bought an island off the most southern point of the coast of Texas, where it joined Mexico. Here he had gone in for raising cattle and hogs and was making his ranch pay fairly well when his brother's letter came. Young Keith was already interested in railroads, of which Texas had at that time only a single forty-mile line between Galveston and Houston. The word of his uncle's exploits was a familiar family saga in which he had always wished himself old enough to play a part. In 1871 he went to join his brother, coming to Puerto Limon on the Atlantic coast. The contract with the Costa Rican government called for the construction of a railway from this point inland to San José, the capital, which was inland on the high, pleasant plateau, nearer the Pacific.

In Costa Rica, as in the other republics, the cities and occupied spaces were toward the Pacific. It was as if the settlers turned their backs on the Atlantic seaboard, and there was reason for so doing. The line of mountains, the Cordillera, lay near the Pacific coast, and on the other side of these mountain ranges, with their many volcanoes, lay broad coastal plains, thick with forest, interwoven with swamps. Today this region has been transformed by banana cultivation, but when Minor Keith arrived, there was no city, or even town or villages at Limon, where stands the beautiful city of the twentieth century. Only a strip of solid ground lay between the ocean and the swamps and jungles which stretched back to the foot of the mountains; and over this waste land it was proposed —it had been decided—to build a railroad up to the city of San José.

The tale of that struggle between man and Nature has never been fully told. Perhaps it never could be. Perhaps it is best that it should not be. In the first year only four miles were built. Keith had gone back to New Orleans and hired men, offering them a dollar a day and food, and had gotten seven hundred, forty of whom had been with Walker in Nicaragua, but most of whom were men picked up on the water front who had neither experience nor reputation. Yet when Keith got them to Limon, they did the work, until the fever struck them down. In three years the road advanced twenty miles, but about that time Henry Keith died in the United States. With his death the contract for the entire work came upon young Minor, who was in that year only twenty-six years old.

If Keith had known that nineteen years were to pass before the railroad actually reached San José, less than one hundred miles away, he would have found it more difficult to endure the trials which beset its building. When that time came, the death toll would have been at least four thousand men, many of whom were skilled young engineers from the States.

But he came to see early that it would be a long time before there was any profitable traffic between the high inland region, with its thick population, and the miles of track which was coming from the seaboard. He cast about in his mind for some business which would bring freight and traffic to his railroad, so that it would begin to make some small return for its enormous costs, and began that industry which was to transform the jungle, the planting of bananas!

PIONEER IN BANANA RAISING

There are different tales of the beginning of the sale of bananas in northern cities. The most authentic is of the steward on a Pacific Mail steamship who bought some of this tropical fruit in a Colombian port and took them to New York, selling them at a profit which surprised him more than it did anyone else. He tried it again, with the same results, and set up a business with his two brothers, who sold the fruits which he brought. That was in 1866 and 1867, and this business of Carl B. Franc and his brothers was well established by the time of the Centennial Exposition in Philadelphia in 1876, where the fruit was on exhibition. A Cape Cod ship captain brought the first bunches of Jamaican bananas to Boston in 1870, and in 1872 Minor Keith, who had never seen a banana until he went on a business trip to Panama, bought from the Carl Franc exporters the first banana bulb to be planted for cultivation in Costa Rica, or, it may be added, in all Central America. He wanted something that would grow in the tropical jungles bordering his new railroad, and was willing to experiment with this newly advertised fruit.

He tested the possible market for the product without waiting for his experimental planting at Limon to come to bearing. On his own account he went out and bought bananas at Colon, and shipped them on a little vessel of his brother's to New Orleans. They sold at a good profit, and he kept on shipping as many bunches as could be sold, sometimes two hundred bunches, sometimes more in a month. They sold at high prices in the States, and he became convinced that there was a future for the fruit.

He began extensive planting of bananas in regions along his railroad which seemed to have suitable conditions for their growth, and thus began to make his railroad bring in returns. "Thus was founded," says the historian of the United Fruit Company, Frederick Upham Adams, "in the deadly jungles of Costa Rica an enterprise which was destined to make these waste lands not only productive but also sanitary. Instead of remaining an enemy, the jungle became a friend—a friend who came bearing gifts of delicious fruit. It was not necessary for the railroad to await the revenue until the peopled plateau was reached. Such waiting would probably have spelled disaster to Mr. Keith. This forcing the jungle to pay tribute was business genius of a high order. It helped to found a gigantic industry, and brought prosperity and an awakening to all of Central America."

MORE RAILROADS

With the extension of the banana industry, Minor Keith looked across the borders of Costa Rica into the neighboring republics and conceived the desire for a great system of inter-related railways which should unite the countries and lead to the Panama railway.

He did much in bringing the railroads of Guatemala

BANANAS GROWING

The industry of banana raising, introduced by Keith, was to
reclaim the jungle lands of the east coast of Central America.

to their high efficiency, and also those of El Salvador. All this was brought about only after cutting his way through endless complications in finance and politics. He had gone to the Mexican border. With the utmost difficulty he completed in 1929 a long line between the two republics of Guatemala and El Salvador, thus creating a system eight hundred miles long. His dream was of continuing this line to the Panama Canal, but death came to him in that year.

HIS SERVICE

No single figure can stand alone in such gigantic undertakings. Others worked with him and along the same lines. Yet the name of Minor Cooper Keith does stand alone as representing the beginning of a new epoch in Central America. No man cared more for an adopted country than he for Costa Rica, and for the larger Central America of which the little republic in which he began his work was a part. He dreamed of its union by railways as other men of a half century earlier had dreamed of that union through political efforts. He came to the country at the time when it was ready to begin its great agricultural development, and stands as a symbol of the changes along those lines which the banana and coffee trade, and the beginning of modern transportation, were to bring. With his projects he and his colleagues created wealth, thus fitting into that Costa Rican spirit suggested, at the head of our chapter, by a French traveler of the past, who said that the Costa Ricans welcomed those bringing wealth from other countries.

At the time of his death the Panama *Star Herald* said, "He was the intimate friend of thousands in these countries, and his intimates were Presidents and Cabinet Ministers, native peons and American negroes. He was the best known North American in Central America, and has done more for the development of these countries by appreciation of their potentialities and faith in their development than any other single man."

BETWEEN OCEANS AND BETWEEN CONTINENTS

BETWEEN OCEANS AND BETWEEN CONTINENTS

"As Europe had formed a Continental System, . . . America should form a system for itself, and assemble by its Representatives . . . whenever circumstances of necessity and great importance should demand it."—Antonio José Canas, 1825.

WHEN we talk of the Americas as one, the picture dates from the early nineteenth century. Its outline was drawn in bold relief by the liberators of South and Central America. England and Europe were interested in Panama and Central America as a bridge between two oceans; but it was only after the yoke of Spain was thrown off that the stretch of "Middle America," running from Mexico City south to the northern boundary of what is now the Republic of Colombia, was seen as a bridge between two continents. That is a thoroughly American picture which was quite unwelcome to England and France and quite contrary to the notions of Spain in those days when her empire was beginning to slip from her grasp. Spain's aim was to hold in her own grasp all colonial trade, forbidding American cities and provinces even to exchange products.

THE PLACE OF PANAMA

Panama was usually the central point in this picture. It had been so from the day in the year 1513 when Balboa stood "upon a peak in Darien," and then went down to the water's edge to take possession of "the newe sea," which he named "Mar del Sur," South Sea. Six years later Pedrarias Davila built a new capital, Panama, on the Pacific (south) coast of the Isthmus, and refounded the town of Nombre de Dios on the northern coast, connecting the two by a path which passed in those days as a "highway." Thus the bridge between the two oceans became a white man's bridge, as it had long been an Indian one in the days of the great Mayan and Aztec civilizations.

The Isthmus of Panama might almost as well have been considered a part of Central America as of South America. It was connected for five years, from 1543 to 1548, with the Captaincy-General of Guatemala, which became after 1821 Central America; but it was soon returned to the great viceroyalty of the south. In the early days it was the starting place for exploring expeditions, and throughout the Spanish occupation was a great center for trade. The convoys coming from Spain to the colonies divided in the Caribbean waters, the ships with cargoes destined for Mexico turning toward a port near Veracruz while all the South American trade was at Nombre de Dios or, later, Puerto Bello, both in Panama.

Here were held the great fairs which gathered hundreds of merchants and traders from the west coast and interior of South America.

Panama began as "Castilla del Oro," Golden Castile, in the smooth-flowing Spanish speech, but the name was soon changed to "Tierra Firme," as a sign of there being this "tierra," land, between the two oceans. So Costa Rica was the "Rich Coast" in the hope of gold and silver to be found there, though it proved to be a poor province until the planting of coffee and the diligent agricultural efforts of its inhabitants brought to it a lasting prosperity.

Guatemala was rightly described by its Mayan (Indian) name meaning "Full of Trees," and Nicaragua, which was explored from Panama by Gil Gonzales Davila, took its name from its Indian chief, Nicaragua or Nicarao. Gonzales rode his horse into the great lake which also bears the chief's name, and was delighted to find the water fresh. He was welcomed with all cordiality by the friendly Indian ruler, who presented him at his departure with a royal gift of cacao beans. The Spaniard returned the courtesy by coming back shortly and taking over the king's possessions and setting his subjects to cultivating, under a system of forced labor which was a virtual slavery, more and more and still more cacao beans. In such fashion did the white man meet such friendly response as they found in these lands.

For a century before the days of independence there was talk of a canal across the Isthmus. French scientists on their way to Peru in 1736 on an errand of measuring the shape of the earth, went home to advise that such a project be undertaken. The Spanish kings planned now and again for such a canal. But it remained to the men of the Wars of Independence to see in Panama a central point for the uniting in friendly and profitable conference, representatives of the different Americas.

A CENTRAL AMERICAN GOES TO WASHINGTON

The name of Antonio José Canas might have been included earlier in our list of leading men of the early days of the republics, if Salvador had not had its Delgado, who led the first movement in Central America for independence, and its man of the same name, Father Simeon Canas, who stood for the abolition of slavery. This second Canas was a younger man, born in 1788, and so one of the youngest members of that distinguished group which met in 1821 to declare for independence. The story of his life gives us one more picture of that thrilling period, and he is the more interesting to us because he was the first Minister permanently accredited by the United Provinces of Central America to the United States.

Born in San Vicente, he taught there, after his university days, in the primary school, living at home with his parents, Don Manuel Mariano Canas and Doña Mariana Asuncion Quintamilla, who both belonged to leading families of Salvador. The charm of manner and frank, open bearing which later made him a welcome guest in the homes of Washington contributed to his success as a teacher. He loved children, and they loved him. To the end of his life he always gathered a group of children around him wherever he was.

Antonio Canas was one of the men who translated his loyalty to the cause of independence into active deeds. When the short-time Emperor of Mexico, Agustín Iturbide, sent General Filisola down into the newly independent Central America to urge and then compel the provinces to come into his empire, Salvador took up arms against the Mexicans, and Antonio Canas took his place in the army. It is remembered that he distinguished himself at the engagement at San Salvador on June 3, 1822.

Canas was one of the men who signed that final decree by the Central American Congress on July 1, 1823, the words of which ring down the years. The provinces, it declared, were "free and independent of Old Spain, of Mexico, and of every other power, whether in the Old or the New World, and they are not, and ought not to be, the patrimony of any Person or Family." These last words are a curious conclusion to the sentence, reflecting the long-time contention of Spain's kings that the colonies were their own personal possessions, with taxes or profits received from them belonging in their private coffers.

Although this decree was published boldly to the world, the new, weak, debt-ridden republics still had some concern—and with good reason—lest the European powers unite to recover such parts as they might of their lost empire. It was a like concern which led President Monroe, on December second of this same year, 1823, to state what became known as the "Monroe Doctrine," in which the objection of the United States to interference in the Americas by European powers was made known.

The friendly support of the United States was more than welcome to the new republic, and one of its first acts was to appoint Don Antonio Canas to represent it at Washington. His credentials were signed by the two men who were holding jointly the presidency, Arcé and Valle. In them he was described as "envoy extraordinary and minister plenipotentiary" of the United Provinces of Central America to the United States. He left immediately after the date of their signing, which was March 30, 1824. Yet he did not reach Washington until early in August.

CANAS DELIVERS AN INVITATION

To Washington in that December of 1824 came the news of the final battle of the South American Wars of Independence. These wars had been going on for nearly fifteen years, and now General Bolívar and his trusted friend General Sucre were sharing in the triumph of this last act, the Battle of Ayacucho. Bolívar was held in great admiration in the United States, where his fortunes had been watched with deep anxiety. The newspapers did not hesitate to call him the "George Washington of South America," and speak openly of American rejoicing in the end of any Spanish dominion on the southern continent.

Bolívar's dream of the future had always gone beyond the mere victory of the colonials over the Spanish armies. In one of the periods when he was in exile, with his cause in apparent defeat, he had written the famous "Letter to the World" in which he spoke of the possible union of the two American continents for purposes of mutual defence and trade relations. A conference at the Isthmus of Panama was even then his goal, for he recognized that this territory between the continents was the neutral meeting place which would be needed in the future. "May we some day be fortunate enough to install there at Panama an august Congress composed of representatives, kings, and empires, that may deal with and discuss the high interests of peace and war with the nations of the other three parts of the world?" he wrote, with that large purpose of his which could go beyond the Americas and take in the entire world.

When the Spanish armies surrendered and the last Spanish official had departed from South American soil, Bolívar moved toward fulfilling his ideal. The United States had recognized his government of Colombia by receiving its diplomat as official representatives at Washington, as it was receiving Don Canas from Central America. In 1822 Bolívar, as President of Colombia, sent communications to several of the other newly independent countries suggesting that they prepare to meet in a Congress to be held at Panama. In December of 1824 he issued invitations to these same States to attend such a conference in 1826, and Colombia's Vice-President, Francisco Santander, in forwarding the communications for his absent President, who was in Peru, added Great Britain, the United States, and Brazil to the list.

Apparently it fell to Canas to deliver this invitation, or, if not, to second it in behalf of the Central American States. We find him making, in November of 1825, a statement to the Secretary of State, Henry Clay, who had worked so long in the House of Representatives for recognition of the southern republics and was considered their best friend in Washington.

"The Government of Central America, as early as 1821, was sensible of the importance to the independent Nations of this Continent, of a General Congress of their Representatives, at some central point, which might consider upon and adopt the best plan for defending the States of the New World from foreign aggression, and, by treaties of alliance, commerce, and friendship, raise them to that elevation of wealth and power, which, from their resources, they may attain. It also acknowledged that as Europe had formed a *Continental System,* and held a Congress whenever questions affecting its interests were to be discussed, America should form a system for itself, and assemble by its Representatives, in Cortés, whenever circumstances of necessity and great importance should demand it."

THE COMING OF THE RAILWAY

With the building of railways between uplands and the coast, Central America began to have a more united life.

Almost one hears the voices of a President and Secretary of State of the mid-twentieth century repeating this statement! Certainly these statesmen would echo other parts of the call to this first Pan American Congress, insisting that the absolute independence of each of the American republics was established, and that the "present neutrality of the United States" would not be compromised by accepting such an invitation. "Will the United States," Canas concluded, "send envoys to the General Congress, the object of which is to preserve and confirm the absolute independence of these Republics and to promote the general good?"

That Congress, as we know, accomplished little. The United States Congress argued and disagreed so long over the appointment of delegates that the men they finally sent started too late. One died on the way to Panama; the other arrived after the company of delegates had adjourned to meet in a Mexican city. Bolívar himself did not manage to attend the gathering. Yet, for all its lack of definite accomplishment, this first Pan American Conference paved the way for later and more successful meetings of the republics of the hemisphere.

TALK OF A CANAL

A letter written by this Minister from Central America to John Quincy Adams, Secretary of State immediately before Henry Clay, discusses a Nicaraguan Canal from ocean to ocean. Canas' description of his country, with which the letter opens, is interesting. It is the "Government of the Republic of the center of America." By it he has been instructed to "promote the opening of a canal in Nicaragua."

Only his nation's poverty prevented the undertaking of such a project. "My Government," he says, "when placed in better circumstances than the present, would not consent to part with the least portion of this distinguished honor." But under the circumstances nothing would be more grateful than the "coöperation of your generous nation, whose noble conduct has been a model and a protection to all the Americas."

Don Canas was forced by ill-health to leave Washington in June of 1826, after slightly less than two years' stay. Years later he became Minister of Foreign Affairs for El Salvador. Twice during the Morazán wars he was head of that State, and 1842 he refused the office of President, desiring to retire to private life. To this his countrymen could not consent. When El Salvador, Honduras, and Nicaragua were attempting, in 1844, a union, they chose him to be its head; but he died in 1844 before his term of office began. When Central America chose him as its first Minister to the United States, it had honored our country by sending one of its most delightful and popular statesmen. The pleasant inter-American relations of those days as of the present depended much on the character of the men who were sent to serve in the capitals of sister republics.

To have a possession over which other more powerful persons quarrel is not a gain for a person; nor does a nation find itself happy in such a position. It was the possession of a possible canal route which made Nicaragua the scene of the Walker-Vanderbilt fight for power, and its territory a matter of contention and treaty making by the United States and Great Britain over a long period of years. When attention was turned to the Panama route by the granting by the Colombians to a French company of the right to build a canal across the Isthmus, the jealousy between the States concerned was revived.

The final choice by the United States of the Panama route in 1903 left Nicaraguans bitterly disappointed. They had seen engineers surveying their country for years, and their hopes had run high of a prosperity which would come from such an undertaking. They still hope that the privilege for a canal which the United States bought from them will be taken up, and that there will be the parallel route with that of Panama. "A land forgotten by the United States," Nicaragua has called itself, but the huge banana plantations carved out of jungle and swamp on its Atlantic coast deny that story. A land of such rich resources will never be forgotten by a hungry world.

INDIANS ALONG THE HIGHWAY

Not till we travel the Pan American Highway, which is now linking the North American continent with the

South American, shall we be able to picture the difficulties which these Central Americans of the early nineteenth century met in setting up their new governments. Nor shall we be able, simply by reading their lives, to catch their enthusiasm for the future of their countries. The story of men can never be told without some understanding of their background, and no nations have been more affected by their geographical position than southern Mexico and the five republics of the "middle land, which is almost a continent in itself."

We can put some of the questions which confronted them to ourselves, even though we cannot fully answer them. What does it do to a man to live in a province which has within its borders every level of land, from sea coast to snow-capped mountain top, so that he can change his climate from the tropics to the temperate zone and then to the frigid by simply traveling a few miles uphill? How can a people be ruled, or rule itself, with no easy way for its mountaineers to go down to its tropics, or its farming population to know its jungle laborers? How can two races come together, the one a thousand years in advance of the other in the ways of the modern world, and work out a new order of life?

As we travel along that highway, we shall take most notice of the Indian people living in their villages and working their fields or those of their employers. The white men found the forefathers of these dark-skinned men and women dwelling in these valleys and on these mountain slopes. There these peoples still live, cheerful and patient in spite of the burdens which were put on their backs and on their hearts by the men who claimed to be their masters.

Twenty-seven million persons are said to live between the Rio Grande and Panama, and by far the greater number of them are Indians or have Indian blood in their veins. Their leaders are often of mixed race, and the old Spanish distinction of caste, against which the Creoles fought in the struggle for independence, has nearly disappeared. The number of Spaniards of pure Castilian blood remaining after these hundreds of years is naturally very small. When we leave Mexico, with its proud Mayan and Aztec and Toltec traditions and ruins, we come first to Guatemala, which is the most Indian of all the republics, with some sixty per cent of its people of practically pure Indian descent, still keeping their native language and customs while modern ways of life are pressing in upon them.

Guatemala is a mountain country, with the highest peaks of any in Central America and a line of volcanoes which tower above its green fields and forests. Today nearly every part of its populated region is to be reached by roads which can be used all the year round. But in the days of the liberators there were only the mule paths whenever one went a short distance out from its cities. It was an adventure for young Barrios to come down from his mountain village to school and college in the city; and

the Indian Carrera could slip back into the mountain re-
treats with his bands of followers and there prepare for
another of his terrifying assaults on towns and cities.

One remembers here in Guatemala a Christian hero
of long ago who loved his people, both Indian and white,
and gave his life to their service. Up in the hills is shown
the birthplace of Barrios; and in the lovely Spanish city of
colonial times, Antigua, which has somehow escaped the
destruction visited on other Spanish cities by volcanic
eruptions, one comes upon the house of Hermano Pedro
and the ruins of his hospital. He was a young Spanish
noble who took vows of the Church and devoted himself
thereafter to the sick and needy. It is told in the old
chronicles how for fifteen years he used to walk the
streets of Antigua at night, jingling his little bell and
praying that its sound might ring in the heart of some
sinner who needed to confess and repent or find some
corner where a sufferer lay in pain. If either call came, he
was ready for it, and in the early morning would often be
seen carrying a sick person on his back to the hospital,
built with the fortune which he had devoted to the
Church. He died in 1667, after his brief fifteen years of
service, but today humble Indian women still come daily
to pray at his tomb.

One sees in every village the church where the priests
gathered the simple, superstitious people. These Indians
were accustomed to having a leader. In the olden days they
had had their chiefs, in the middle days, the church fa-

thers. The white men who conquered them in the long-ago centuries made themselves their masters, and from that day to this the dark-skinned people have worked for other people. In the nineteenth century they accepted the rule of the typical Central American "strong man," whether liberator or dictator, and did not look farther. No liberator was allowed time to educate them or train them in the simplest beginnings of democracy.

"NATURAL ALLIES OF DEMOCRACY"

An American "observer" of the present year, Mr. R. H. Markham, has come to the conclusion, after traveling through Mexico and Central America, that these Indians of the working classes are, as he puts it, the "natural allies of democracy." "There is no rigid racial line between the various groups," he says. "An Indian is not excluded from high social, political, or military positions, at least in theory. But, in reality, he is the underprivileged. . . . An Indian usually works for other people, often for twenty cents a day or less. He takes the poor land, which the richest people do not consider worth exploiting. In certain countries he pays practically all the taxes. . . . He carries loads, greater than any other people that I have ever seen except the Ethiopians. An Indian trots for days up and down hills with loads weighing scores of pounds upon his back, held by a broad strap tugging against his forehead. He carries more than a donkey can. Donkeys absolutely refuse to do what the Indians do."

As he journeyed up and down these lands, Mr. Markham met these Indians in many places, transporting every sort of load. In Guatemala City he saw an elderly man stop before a splendid mounted statue of a great Guatemalan liberator and let his burden rest on the base of the monument. Had he been liberated? One wondered. His enormous sack of grain was so heavy that Mr. Markham could hardly lift it, much less carry it. "They trot along in rain and shine," he continues. "They ford rivers and cross very high ridges. They carry their merchandise as far as fifty miles to market. At night I saw them stretched out, silent and weary in the dark, reclining on mats, sheltered, if fortunate, by some porch roof. Their food was cold cornmeal pancakes, with pepper; perhaps a little cheese, maybe fruit, sometimes beans. Of such persons are formed Mexico and the Central American nations. These are 'the people.' They tend the corn, care for the coffee, gather most of the fruit, do the hard work on buildings, make the roads. . . . As one sojourns among these somewhat stolid, good-natured, very hardy people, he cannot but wonder whether they . . . tend toward absolutism or democracy."

The answer seemed to him very plain. "They are classical enemies," he declares, "of central regimentation and of one-man dictatorship. They are our natural allies and natural friends. By means of their astounding fortitude and heroic resistance through four long, hard centuries,

—: 268 :—

they have resisted, survived, and partially overcome one of the world's worst tyrannies. Their aims are our aims."

IN FOUR REPUBLICS

Honduras and El Salvador are next southward beyond Guatemala along the great Pan American Highway, Honduras being the third largest of the Central American States, and El Salvador, along the Pacific coast, the smallest. Honduras has always suffered politically from outsiders. Its colonial life lay on its Pacific side with Tegucigalpa, a beautiful Spanish city, as its capital and as the center for the gold region which made this province, in Spanish eyes, the most important part of Central America. On the Atlantic side its harbors and forests of dyewoods and mahogany attracted the freebooters of the Caribbean. For centuries Great Britain disputed possession of this coast with Spain, leaving the Hondurans little to say about these unexplored lands. Today the Atlantic coast is a great banana country. The traveler finds it still thinly populated, but rich in resources which the present century will doubtless see developed. Here the Indian racial type is mingled with the negro, making a caste of so-called "zambos." A slave ship wrecked on the coast in the seventeenth century, and a stream of fugitive slaves from the West Indies are responsible for this blending of the races.

El Salvador has been called a "tropical garden." It is

the only republic which lies wholly on one ocean instead of reaching across the Isthmus. Here the Indian people cultivate the farms and the coffee plantations. Through general education the children are coming into some idea of the ways of a modern republic and will become more intelligent citizens than their fathers had the opportunity to be.

In Nicaragua the Indian element predominates. From the earliest times there has been much intermarrying, and there is therefore a large mixed population. Here the occupations of the workers are varied, according to the character of the country. There are broad plains, with herds of cattle and horses and mules, and plantations with many crops, including coffee, cacao, sugar, tobacco, rice and indigo. A glance at the map shows the lakes and rivers which make this region different from that of the republics which border it to the north and south.

Costa Rica, next southward and adjoining Panama, has a population made up largely of the white race, descendants of the Spanish colonists. They live in beautiful, semitropical surroundings, and seem to the traveler more modern in their ways than the people away from the highroads in some of the other republics.

High in the mountains of Costa Rica one may see the ancient Indian trail, which went through a pass ten thousand feet above sea level, and was approached on either side through wooded or jungle regions. Along this path the Indians of long ago passed from North to South

GOVERNMENT BUILDING IN SAN SALVADOR
Capital of the Republic of El Salvador.

America. Their mode of travel was by land. To them, as to modern Americans, the Isthmus was a bridge between the two lands, whereas to the white men, who came to America in boats, it was for centuries considered a barrier between the two oceans.

INDEPENDENCE DAYS

INDEPENDENCE DAYS

"A people may be judged by its holidays and its heroes."

TO leave our story of Mexico and Central America without a mention of fiestas would be impossible. Our "liberators and heroes" are known to the people of their own countries not through books or even the spoken word, much as the Latin Americans like speech making, but through the yearly Independence Day celebrations. These holidays bring to life these heroes of whom we have been telling, giving color and reality to these men of the past whose statues stand in the plazas and whose names have been taken by cities and towns and broad avenues. Those are cold memorials, good in their way, but not after the Spanish-Indian tradition, which demands a fiesta, a happy, national day of gaiety and church going and speech making.

More than most peoples the Mexicans and Central Americans cherish in their festivals their picturesque past. Strangers never cease to marvel at the way the tragic days of the conquistadores are recalled in dances and pageants, in which Indians take not only the parts of the members of their own race but the roles of their oppressors, enacting the scenes of the conquest with a memory only of their drama and not of their horror. So anyone who is fortunate in being in any of these republics on a national holiday commemorating independence will find the events of the nineteenth century recalled with popular rejoicing.

IN MEXICO

Mexico has for its Independence Day the Sixteenth of September with which our story began, when the President of the Republic rings the Liberty Bell in the National Palace in Mexico City, and all over the separate States of the nation the people gather in churches and public plazas to recall the *Grito de Dolores* and Miguel Hidalgo, "Father of Mexican Independence," who sounded forth that famous call to freedom on that early morning of the year 1810. Mexico has also its Guadalupe Day, December Twelfth, which is especially an Indian holiday, recalling the appearance of the Virgin of Guadalupe to the humble Indian on the hillside. That, too, is tied in with the winning of independence, for the banner of Guadalupe was carried at the head of the Indian companies which swarmed after Father Hidalgo.

Another national holiday, Constitution Day, February Fifth, recalls the time of Benito Juarez. On that day in 1857 the constitution was proclaimed which gave back to the people many personal liberties of the early days of independence that had been lost during the long dictatorship of Santa Anna. This document, which also abolished many monopolies and special Church privileges, marked the beginning of the War of Reform in which Juarez was the chief figure.

To the modern Mexican Juarez stands as the representative figure of democracy. In all his dealings he was honest, and in all his holding of public office he was completely untouched by the opportunities which his position gave for personal profit. Nor did he permit any man of all his patriot group to gain wealth at the expense of the people's treasury. Juarez was not a military man, and he did not try to assume all the offices of the government, as was the dictator custom. He appointed generals to lead the armies and left the task to them, although he was always their chief. The battle for reform was his battle, and he fought it for fifteen years, whether in the law courts over which he presided or in the halls of Congress or on the battlefields. It was his devotion which held the people steadily to that aim. When the Mexicans celebrate their Constitution Day, they are honoring the memory of an Indian President who stood for the progressive measures which were too advanced for his own day but are being adopted in the present century.

IN GUATEMALA

Guatemala joins the other republics in celebrating September Fifteenth, a day which its people feel to be particularly theirs because the signing of the Declaration of Independence took place in its capital. That Declaration marked the separation of Central America from Spain.

Its other national day belongs to itself alone. June Thirtieth is the anniversary of the 1871 revolution which followed the death of Carrera and the end of his long dictatorship. On that day they remember their Barrios, who is to them what Washington or Lincoln are to us. He started their nation on the modern road, beginning to introduce the reforms which, as in the case of other liberators, were in advance of his time.

When we of North America think of Barrios, we like to remember that he believed in friendly relations with the United States. Important speeches which he made in the later years of his administration urge upon his people a willingness to accept foreign help in developing the country's resources. He wanted the Nicaraguan Canal built, with American capital if need be, and endeavored to restore the Union of Central American Republics. He was a modern person in his ambitions. Who can forget the picture of him sitting in the cab of the locomotive which he had imported, exhibiting proudly to his people this newest invention?

Guatemala had always had government by "strong men," either in the role of dictator or as "constitutional president." From the days of Spanish rule its people were accustomed to such leadership. In recent years it has been called the "paternalistic republic" because of this continuing tendency. Yet its leaders declare that they are exercising their present authority in the interest of future democracy.

HONDURAS AND ITS MORAZÁN

In a similar way the Republic of Honduras honors
Morazán, making his birthday, October third, their national day. Other republics of Central America may
rightfully claim their share in this liberator, who worked
and fought at the head of the Liberals for the good of all
the countries; but by birth and home ties Morazán belongs
to Honduras. His day and the familiar September Fifteenth of the Declaration of Independence from Spain
are its national holidays, celebrated each year by young
and old.

Honduras clings, too, to its Indian traditions, honoring
the chief, Lempira, who opposed the Spanish conquest,
along with the later "liberators."

IN NICARAGUA

Nicaragua makes another and an interesting choice.
Along with its Independence Day of September it has
decided, within recent years, to join with the South American republics in observing the birthday of the great Liberator, Simon Bolívar, the Twenty-Fourth of July. Any
Latin-American republic does well to honor him, for his
was the guiding hand which led the colonies along the
path of freedom. Central America would have been unable to slip from Spanish control with hardly any blood
shed if the armies of Bolívar had not been winning their
decisive victories from Venezuela to Peru.

EL SALVADOR

El Salvador, always independent and a law unto itself, has its own special Independence Day, as well as sharing the general Central American celebration of September Fifteenth in memory of the year 1821. It had its heroes all along the way, with its Delgado leading the first revolt against Spanish rule in 1811, ten years before the Guatemala Declaration, and its armies resisting with force the annexation to Mexico of 1822. In 1841 the little republic became weary of the strife between its sister republics and declared itself an independent and sovereign nation. That second Independence Day, November Fifth of 1841, is remembered each year with holiday making and national celebration in this tiny, peaceful, progressive State.

IN COSTA RICA

Last of them all comes Costa Rica, with its September Fifteenth, and also its April Eleventh. That is the day of the Battle of Rivas, when Mora and his army fought on Nicaraguan soil against William Walker and his men for the freedom of Central America from foreign intervention. It is the day of its young hero who snatched up the flaming torch and set fire to the building that sheltered the enemy, knowing that he did it at the cost of his life. Every Costa Rican joins with enthusiasm in the patriotic demonstrations of that anniversary.

TWO OTHER DAYS

Two more days are added to the holiday calendar of these republics, days in which the United States and the South American republics join. One is the day of the discovery of America, October Twelfth, our Columbus Day, which is known in these countries as the "Day of the Race." There is no country where it is not remembered with celebration, and the air is filled with messages of unity and good will, as anyone who turns on his radio can prove. Latterly another day is likewise a good will day, April Fourteenth, Pan American Day, celebrated officially in Washington and every other capital of the twenty-one republics, and gaining in importance each year. All our "liberators and heroes" would have joined gladly in the demonstrations of that day, for they had the vision of the united Americas for which it stands.

NOTES

HINTS FOR PRONUNCIATION

FOR a full guide to proper pronunciation a Spanish dictionary or grammar should be consulted. But lest our tongues make too heavy work of the beautiful, liquid vowels and the soft consonants, we list a few of the points to be noted as differing from our English naming of persons and places.

Vowel sounds should be given as follows: a as in *far*, e as in *den*, i as in *machine*, o as in *Norse*, u as in *rule*, and y, when it stands alone, like the *i* in *machine*.

Applying these rules, we sound the a as in *far* in the names of Hidalgo, Galvez, Mora, the e in Morelos as in *den*, and the y (meaning "and") in Hidalgo y Costilla like the *i* in *machine*. The ll in Costilla is pronounced as if it were the *lli* in the word *billion*. A similar sounding of the letter i comes in the word *grito*, which would sound more as if it were spelled with a double *ee* if it were not that the vowel is touched more lightly.

When we come to consonants, we must always remember that the letter *j* is pronounced not as in our proper name John, but like a strongly aspirate English h. This changes completely the sound of the name Juarez, or of the common name of José, so frequently borne by our patriots. The same sound for j, as like our *h*, holds in the middle of a place-name like Guadalajara. In the place-name Queretaro, and elsewhere, qu is sounded like our *k,* and at the end of the alphabet the Spanish American way of sounding z is like our *s,* or really like our *ss,* as, for instance, in Zamora, or Zapotec.

Considering words as a whole, we note that all the letters of a Spanish name (except h, which is always silent) are always sounded. The final e, thus, is sounded in Iturbide; or in Valle. The other rule which helps here is that words ending in a vowel, as Iturbide or Valle or Costilla, or in the consonants n or s, are accented on the next to the last syllable, while all others are stressed on the final syllable, *except when otherwise marked.* That last phrase brings out the reason for the accents so often placed above the vowels. They are to guide us away from the pronunciation which would be used according to these rules. So José, though ending in a vowel, is accented on the final syllable, and Morazán given a similar stress in spite of its final n.

These few suggestions do no more than skim the surface of this subject; but they will serve their purpose if they prevent the complete Anglicizing of these names and turn the interest to a further study of the language which we shall meet all along the Pan American highway.

A LATIN AMERICAN CALENDAR
OF INDEPENDENCE

NO colony of the Spanish American empire won its freedom alone. The weakness of the home government and the revolts of native Americans on a front which stretched from Mexico to the southern provinces of South America brought about, in a period of years, the withdrawal of Spanish officials and troops from the Americas. The events in Mexico and Central America should, therefore, be fitted into the larger picture. The revolution took place in three main efforts, in northern South America, under Miranda, Bolívar, and their associates, in southern South America, under San Martín, Artigas, Belgrano, O'Higgins, and in Mexico, under Hidalgo, Morelos, and Iturbide. Central America slipped out from Spanish control practically without bloodshed. In each region there were preliminary uprisings, but the impetus was given by the entry of Napoleon into Spain.

1808: Napoleon's troops in Spain and Portugal; Joseph Bonaparte on the Spanish throne; flight of royal family of Portugal to Brazil.

April, 1810: Spanish captain-general expelled from Caracas, Venezuela.

May, 1810: Declaration of Independence in Buenos Aires, Argentina.

A CALENDAR OF INDEPENDENCE

September, 1810: *Grito de Dolores,* Mexico; revolution led by Hidalgo, Allende.

September, 1810: Declaration of Independence in Chile.

July, 1811: Declaration of Independence of Venezuela.

July, 1811: Execution of Hidalgo.

November, 1811: Revolt in San Salvador, led by Delgado.

November, 1813: Declaration of Independence of Mexico (Morelos).

1814: First Constitution of Mexico; defeat and death of Morelos.

1821: Plan of Iguala (Iturbide); Mexico declares itself a sovereign nation.

1821: Declaration of Independence by Central America at Guatemala.

1822: *Grito do Ypiranga,* Brazil.

1823: Constitution of independent Central America.

1823: Monroe Doctrine pronounced.

1824: Battle of Ayacucho, final victory of South American Wars of Independence.

BIBLIOGRAPHY

THE following list of books is by no means a complete source list for this volume, for such a listing would contain the names of books, pamphlets, and magazine articles in both English and Spanish which would be either difficult to obtain or of no special interest to the general reader. The pertinent information has been extracted for use in the brief biographies, and they have thus served their purpose. It is a general reading list for those who wish to carry the study of these men, their times and their countries further, and is included in the hope that this may be done, for the limitations of a biographical treatment leave opportunities for such browsing in the field.

GENERAL HISTORIES

Fitzgibbon, Russell H., Visual Outline of Latin American History. New York, 1938. An inexpensive volume of the Students Outline Series, which is valuable in locating briefly and accurately in paragraph summaries both people and events.

Chapman, Charles Edward, Colonial Hispanic America. New York, 1933; Republican Hispanic America. New York, 1937. Chapter VII is on "The Age of Caudillos."

Bancroft, Hubert Howe. Works (39 v. 1882-1891). History

of Mexico, Volumes IV to VI. History of Central America, Volume III. A repository of valuable information.

Kirkpatrick, F. A., Latin America. A Brief History. London and New York, 1939. (Quotation from, on back of end-paper.)

MEXICO

Bancroft, H. H., History of Mexico, IV, chaps. 1, 2, 5-19, 39-41 (Hidalgo to Iturbide period); V, chaps. 1-6, 11-13 (Iturbide to Juarez period).

Fisher, Lillian E., The Background of the Revolution for Mexican Independence. Boston, 1934.

Fortier, Alcée, and Ficklen, John Rose, Central America and Mexico. London and Philadelphia, 1907. (Being Volume Nine of the History of North America).

Priestley, Herbert Ingram, The Mexican Nation, a History. New York, 1925.

Zabre, Alfonso Teja, Guide to the History of Mexico: A Modern Interpretation. Mexico, 1935. (Quotations from, pages 211, 217-218).

Noll, Arthur Howard, A Short History of Mexico. Chicago, 1903; From Empire to Republic: The Story of the Struggle for Constitutional Government in Mexico. Chicago, 1903.

Gruening, Ernest, Mexico and Its Heritage. New York and London, 1928.

Winter, Nevin O., Mexico and Her People of Today. Boston, 1907.

Simpson, Lesley Byrd, Many Mexicos. New York, 1941.

CENTRAL AMERICA

Fortier, Alcée, and Ficklen, John Rose, Central America and Mexico. (See above).

BIBLIOGRAPHY

Koebel, W. H. Central America. New York, 1918.

Munro, Dana Gardner, The Five Republics of Central America: their political and economic development and their relations with the United States. New York, 1918.

Ruhl, Arthur Brown. The Central Americans: Adventures and Impressions between Mexico and Panama. New York and London, 1928.

Thompson, Wallace, Rainbow Countries of Central America. New York, 1926.

Rothery, Agnes, Central America and the Spanish Main. Boston, 1929.

Crowther, Samuel, The Romance and Rise of the American Tropics. New York, 1929.

Adams, Frederick Upham, Conquest of the Tropics. New York, 1914. (Quotation from, page 248).

COUNTRY BY COUNTRY

Travels

Lyon, Capt. G. F., Journal of a Residence and Tour in the Republic of Mexico, in the Year 1826. London, 1828. (Quotations from, pages 28-29, 40-41).

Wells, William V., Explorations and Adventures in Honduras. New York, 1857. (Quotations from, pages 168-170).

Poinsett, Joel Roberts, Notes on Mexico, 1822. Philadelphia, 1924. (Quotations from, pages 70-71).

Stephens, John Lloyd, Incidents of Travel in Central America, Chiapas, and Yucatan. New York, 1841. (Quotations from, pages 125, 129-132, 155).

Description

Fergusson, Erna, Guatemala. New York, 1937.

Burbank, Addison, Guatemala Profile, New York, 1939.

Winter, Nevin O., Guatemala and Her People of Today. Boston, 1909.

BIBLIOGRAPHY

Martin, Percy Falcke, Salvador of the Twentieth Century. London and New York, 1911.

Jones, Chester Lloyd, Costa Rica and Civilization in the Caribbean. Wisconsin, 1935.

Walker, J. W. G., Ocean to Ocean. 1898. (Nicaragua).

Cramer, Floyd, Our Neighbor Nicaragua, 1929.

Markham, R. H., South of the Rio Grande. Series, Christian Science Monitor, Aug., Sept., 1941. (Quotation from, pp. 267-269).

Biography

Robertson, William Spence, Rise of the Spanish American Republics as told in the lives of their liberators. New York and London, 1918.

Noll, Howard, and McMahon, A. Philip, The Life and Times of Miguel Hidalgo y Costilla. Chicago, 1810.

Iturbide, Agustin de, Political Life of the Ex-Emperor of Mexico, Written by Himself. . . . 1823. London, 1827.

Burgess, Paul, Justo Rufino Barrios. Philadelphia, 1926.

Scroggs, William Oscar, Filibusters and Financiers: the story of William Walker and his associates. New York, 1916. (Quotation from, page 189).

Greene, Laurence, The Filibuster: the career of William Walker, 1937. (Quotations from, pages 163, 178).

Burke, Ulick Ralph, A Life of Benito Juarez, constitutional president of Mexico. London and Sydney, 1894. (Quotation from, page 205).

For brief biographical articles on Central American heroes, see Pan American Bulletin, as indexed in its volumes and in the Readers' Guide to Periodical Literature.

INDEX

LIBERATORS AND HEROES OF SOUTH AMERICA

By MARION LANSING

Jacket in full color by Paul Quinn. Also illustrated from photographs $3.00

Some thirty years after the American Colonies had gained their independence from England, South America began her long and bloody struggle for freedom from the yoke of Spain. And just as the American Revolution gave us such great names as Paul Revere and Samuel Adams, so the Wars of Independence gave to South America the great national heroes whom she honors today.

Simón Bolívar, often called the "George Washington of South America" was, of course, the supreme genius of the Wars of Independence, but there were many others, of whom little is known, who played their part no less magnificently. Among them are: Miranda, Forerunner of Independence; San Martín, Savior of the South; Moreno, Champion of Free Speech; O'Higgins, Supreme Director of Chile; Santander, Man of Laws; and Paez, The Man on Horseback.

. . . "In this series of sixteen biographical sketches, Marion Lansing tells the story of the men who made possible these South American countries of today. It is a book of substance and style. It comprises a single story, and a great one it is, of sacrifice, devotion, adventure and the highest courage, one to be read and remembered wherever freedom is prized." . . . *New York Times.*

. . . "These sixteen biographies of South American heroes are the type of literature that will further Pan Americanism, for a knowledge of the history of a people and how it parallels our own aids in bringing understanding.

"Parallels there are, and described vividly. . . . Ragged troops that suffered terrors equal to Valley Forge, and battles as thrilling as Bunker Hill. And through it all the same desire for freedom from overseas tyrants." . . . *Philadelphia Record.*

My Jungle Trails

BY *A. HYATT VERRILL*

*Illustrated from photographs and paintings by the author and
Charles Livingston Bull* $3.50

A. Hyatt Verrill's knowledge of Latin American jungles *is
probably unexcelled by that of any scientist-explorer in the
United States today,* writes Professor Kirtley F. Mather in
recommending MY JUNGLE TRAILS for THE SCIENTIFIC BOOK
CLUB, and he adds:

"Mr. Verrill's tales are far from humdrum and commonplace. He is
an expert raconteur and he has selected from his rich store many
vivid experiences that *hold the reader's interest as surely as the year's
best detective story.* More than that, they are a means of insight into
the ways of nature and man in tropical lowlands, which is far more
realistic than that gained from the usual geographic or ethnological
treatise.

"Even the city-bred must sense the lure of the jungles as he reads this
splendid collection of narratives. . . . Adventures of all sorts are the
inevitable by-products of the quests for rare animals or plants or for
information concerning strange peoples beyond the frontiers of civilization. Perhaps it is because Mr. Verrill has sought something other
than adventure that his narration rings so true."

MY JUNGLE TRAILS is based upon Mr. Verrill's experiences
and adventures gained during nearly fifty years in which as
naturalist, ethnologist, author and artist he has led expeditions into the unknown jungles of Darien, the "forbidden"
districts of the Kunas in Panama, and followed the jungle
creeks and trails of British Guiana and all the other countries
of equatorial America.

"As Mr. Verrill looks back over almost half a century, this veteran
wanderer finds adventurous tales to tell. He has brought together
what are frankly the most unusual things that have happened to him
to make a very interesting book. In strange hinterlands of Panama
and Costa Rica, in Santo Domingo and the Lesser Antilles, and in
the mysterious fastnesses of British Guiana, the author met with incidents which were sometimes exciting, sometimes amusing, sometimes puzzling and almost always unpredictable. The result is a variety which never lets the reader down."—*New York Herald-Tribune.*

Included in the AMERICAN LIBRARY ASSOCIATION BOOKLIST

The Pan American Highway, beginning at Laredo, Texas, has 3297 miles to cover before it reaches Panama. Of these there are 300 miles in Guatemala, 180 in El Salvador, 90 through Honduras, 250 in Nicaragua, 350 in Costa Rica. Portions of this road are completed but other portions are still only "dry weather roads," and brief sections at the most difficult points are still trails through the jungle. Each republic is, however, making efforts to complete its section. Information on its progress may be obtained from the Public Roads Administration, Washington, D.C.

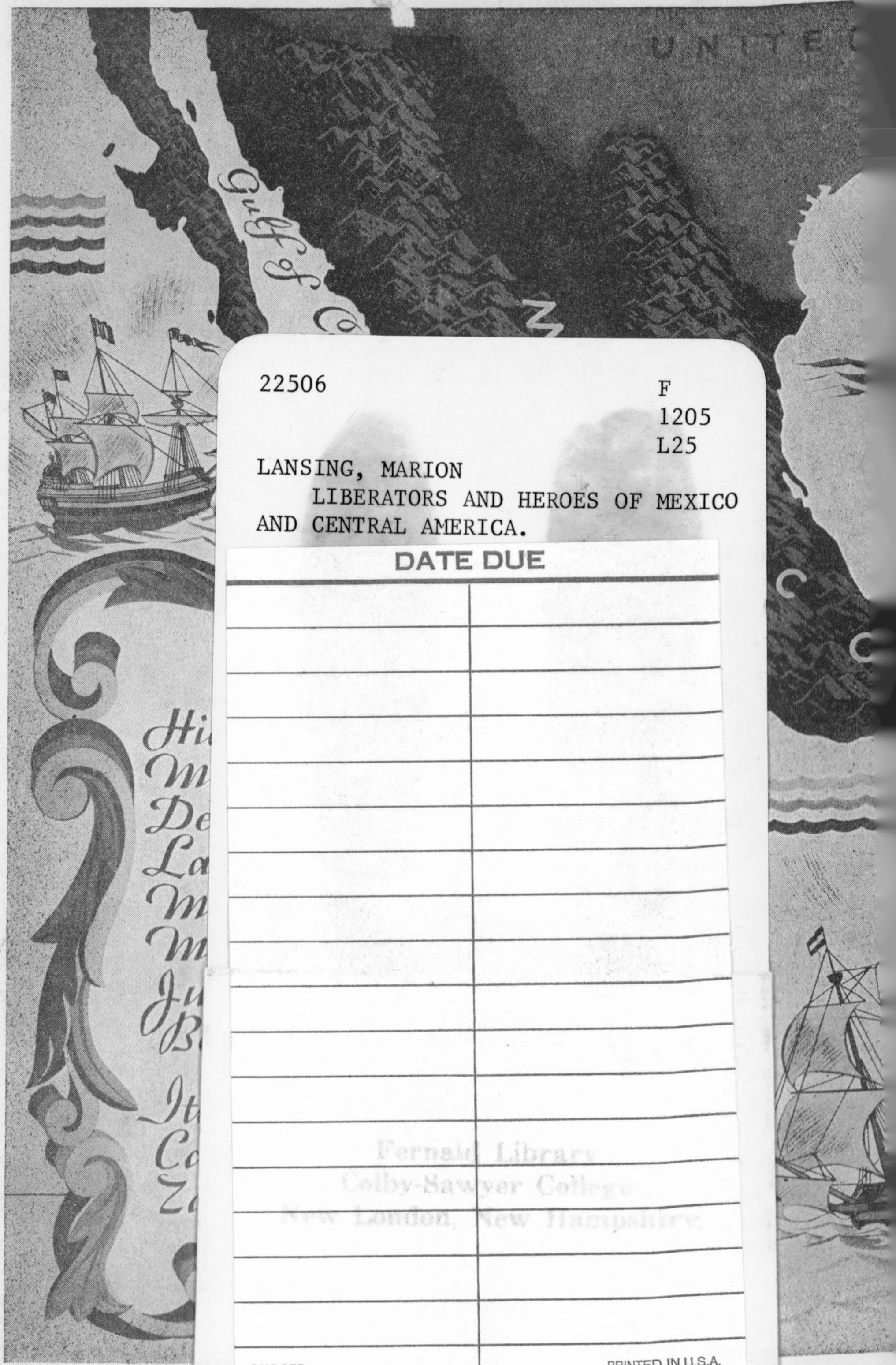